Simple Paper Craft

SIMPLE
PAPER CRAFT

Gunvor & Harriet Ask

B. T. Batsford Ltd London
Charles T. Branford Company Newton Mass.

First English language edition 1971
7134 2293 9
Branford SBN 1–8231–7020–9
Library of Congress Catalog Card Number: 72 131435
Reprinted 1973

Printed by The Anchor Press Ltd, and bound by
William Brendon & Son Ltd, both of Tiptree, Essex,
for the publishers
B. T. Batsford Ltd.
4 Fitzhardinge Street, London W.1, and
Charles T. Branford Company
28 Union Street, Newton Centre, Massachusetts 02159

CONTENTS

Gnomes and a decorated Christmas tree

The tree is cut from duplicating paper. Trace the tree onto a folded sheet of paper so that the dotted line lies on the fold. Now lay three or four sheets of duplicating or tracing paper under the folded piece and sew along the dotted line with your sewing-machine. Leave enough cotton to fasten off at each end of the seam so that it does not come undone. Fold the paper back along the seam and cut the tree out with a pair of sharp, pointed scissors, not too large. Unfold the tree. When all the leaves are separated and spread out round the

seam, the tree will stand up, lovely and bushy, with its decorations and its star.

The gnomes are cut from paper folded accordion fashion, but into no more than four, or it will be too thick to cut. Transfer the shape onto the folded paper, with the dotted lines along the folds. Cut it out, and the row of gnomes is ready. If you want it longer, cut out another set and stick it on firmly with a pair of little triangular flaps at hand and foot.

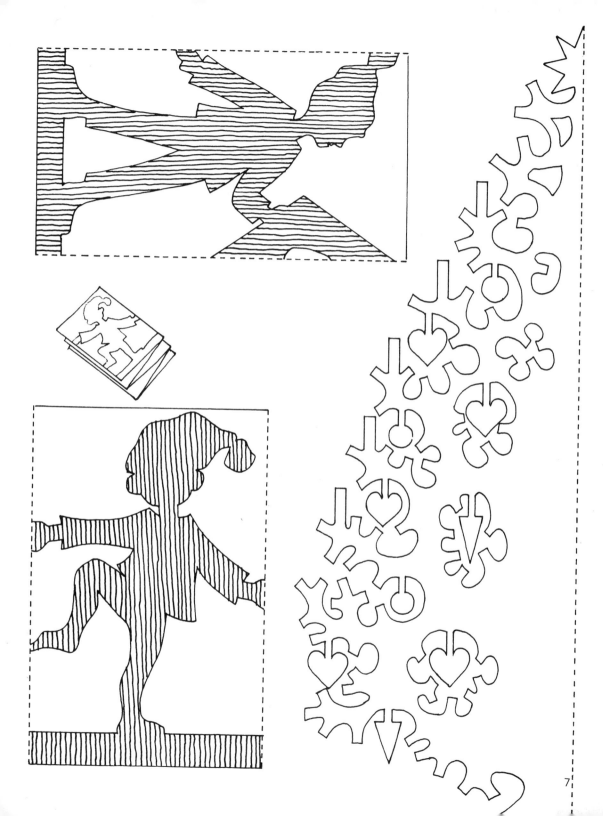

Reindeer with sleigh and fir trees

Transfer the reindeer onto a piece of strong paper, folded so that both sides are cut out at the one time. Stick together the head sections and halfway down the body but not the antlers. Bend the legs and the antlers outwards and the reindeer will stand up.

If the sleigh is to carry little parcels, you must cut it out of cardboard. Transfer the sleigh shape onto the folded cardboard so that the upper dotted line lies on the fold. Cut the sleigh out, and bend the sides downwards so that it stands. Fix the front runners together by the little triangular flaps. The parcels are made of tiny pieces of cardboard, wrapped in brightly-coloured gloss paper.

Stick them onto the sleigh firmly.

The trees are made of white duplicating or tracing paper. Transfer the tree shape onto a folded piece of paper, so that the dotted line lies on the fold. Lay three or four sheets of duplicating or tracing paper under the one with the drawing on it, and sew along the dotted line with your sewing-machine. Leave enough cotton thread to fasten off at the top and bottom of the seam so that it does not come undone. Fold the paper back around the seam and cut out the tree with a pair of sharp, pointed scissors, not too large. Unfold the tree. When all the layers are separated and spread out, the tree will stand up, lovely and bushy.

9

Spiral Christmas tree

If you make the spiral Christmas tree according to our diagram, it will measure about $5\frac{1}{2}$ inches in height. It is made of thin white cardboard, and consists of two parts: a cone, and a strip, 4 feet 4 inches long, which you can make by sticking several strips together. The diagram for the cone is full size. Transfer it onto cardboard, cut it out and stick the straight edges together. Draw the long strip according to the diagram and cut it out. Now stick it to the cone, beginning at the top and spiralling downwards. Use just enough paste for one round at a time, and hold the pieces firm until the paste is dry. The dotted areas on the diagram show where to apply the paste.

1″

4′ 4″

$1\frac{3}{4}″$

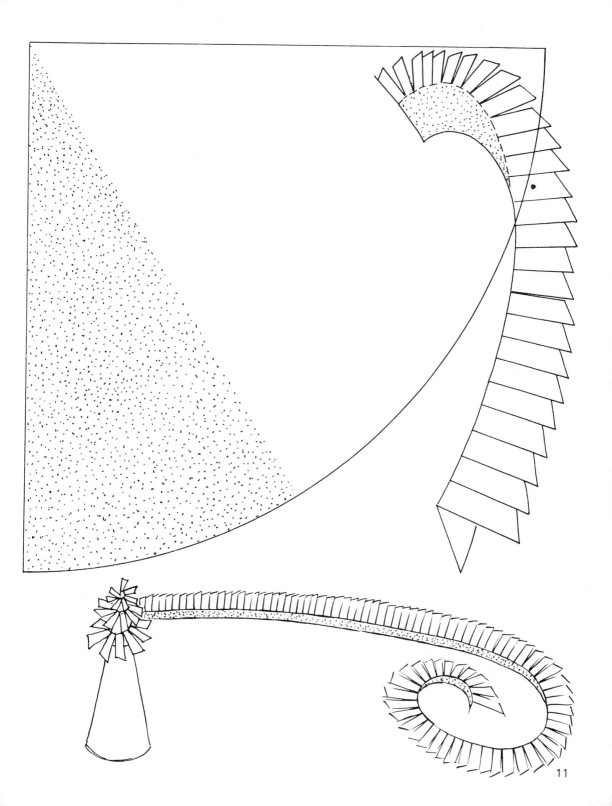

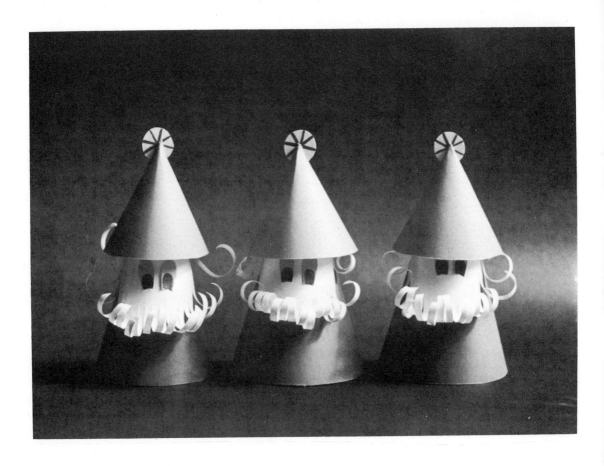

Father Christmas table decorations

The diagram on the facing page is full size, and the dotted areas show where to apply the paste. The body and hood of the Father Christmas are each made of a cone, the body in pillar-box red, the hood in orange. The beard is made of thin white notepaper and the tassel of white cardboard with radiating stripes drawn on it. First, stick up the body cone, adding a strip of sticky tape on the inside. Next, cut out the beard and curl it by drawing each strand between your index finger and the edge of a plastic ruler. Draw the eyes onto the beard, and stick it on firmly, holding it extra-fast at the back with a piece of sticky tape (see the small diagram). Stick up the hood, and set it on top of the body cone. With a sharp knife, cut a slit through both head and body cones, which will now be held together by the tassel disc, pushed right down into the slit.

A package for bon-bons

Make the Father Christmas large enough to carry a small present of sweets under the body cone.

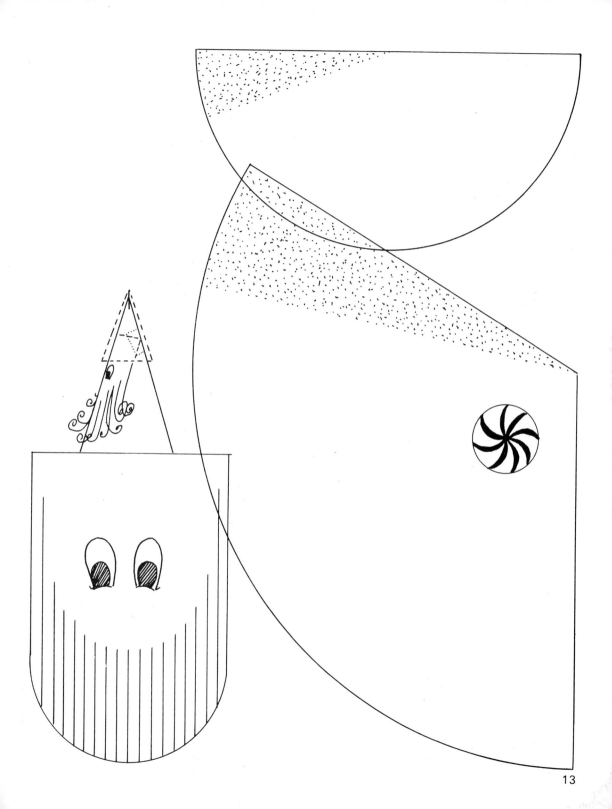

13

Choir girls

A paper doily is a splendid material for making figures, but a circular lacy cut-out is just as good, though it should, in this case, be finished off with a border. Form the paper into a cone and stick it. Push a cocktail-stick into a Styrofoam ball painted pink and then down through the tip of the cone. Wind a few strands of mercerized embroidery thread round four fingers, put a little paste on the head, front and back, and smooth the hair on. Stick on the arms and hands, and provide each singer with a book. Now they are ready. The window is cut out of folded paper, with the fold on the dotted line. Cut out and unfold the paper. In the photo, the girls are standing on a circle of cardboard, 9 inches in diameter backed by a curved sheet of corrugated paper, 12 inches high. Before you stick the window onto the corrugated paper, stick a piece of coloured paper behind the window-frame to look like stained-glass.

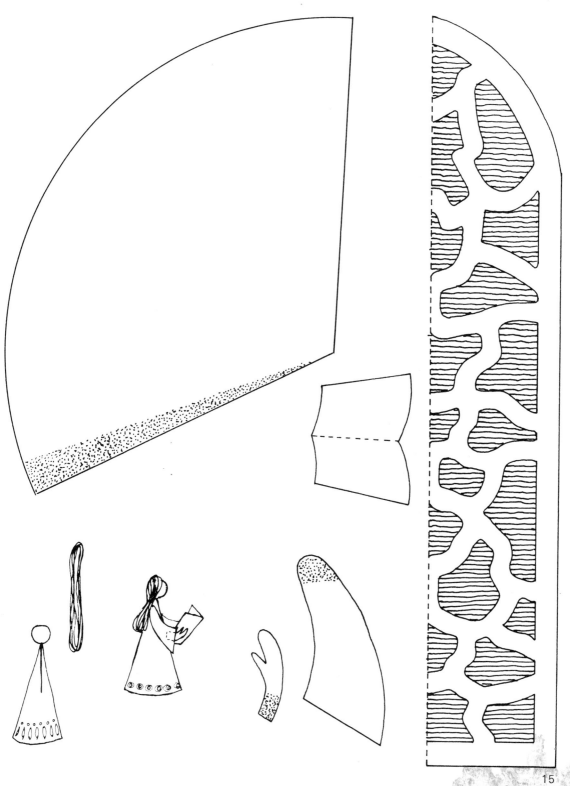

A basket from a star

The diagram is full size. Make this basket of gloss paper or metal foil. Transfer the star onto the paper and cut it out. Along the dotted lines nearer the centre, fold each point so that it sticks straight up into the air when the base is flat on the table. A strip of the same paper, $8 \times \frac{1}{2}$ inches, is stuck around the points, against the outer dotted line, as in the small diagram. Now fold the points downward, over the strip. Fasten a handle, $8 \times \frac{1}{2}$ inches, onto the inner side of the basket.

Fringed cone

The diagram is full size. Trace the diagram onto gloss paper or metal foil. Cut it out and curl the fringes. Stick the cone up, and fasten a handle firmly to the inside.

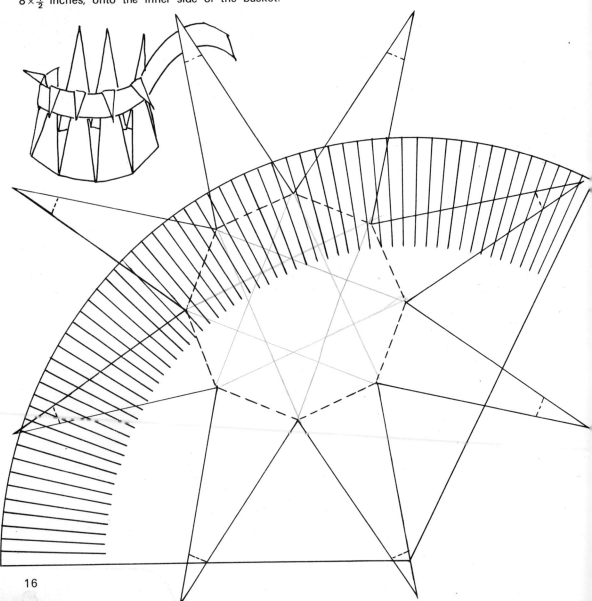

An expanded cone

This little diagram is half-size, except for the one point that has been drawn to show you the full size. Trace the small diagram onto parchment paper, and enlarge the points, so that all four are the right size, using the centre line as a guide. Now transfer the shape onto gloss paper or metal foil and cut it out. Score along the dotted line, fold, and stick together so that the points are turned outwards. The tips of the points, folded as shown in the diagram, are stuck firmly onto the bottom point of the cone. Fix a handle, $8 \times \frac{1}{2}$ inches, securely to the inside of the cone.

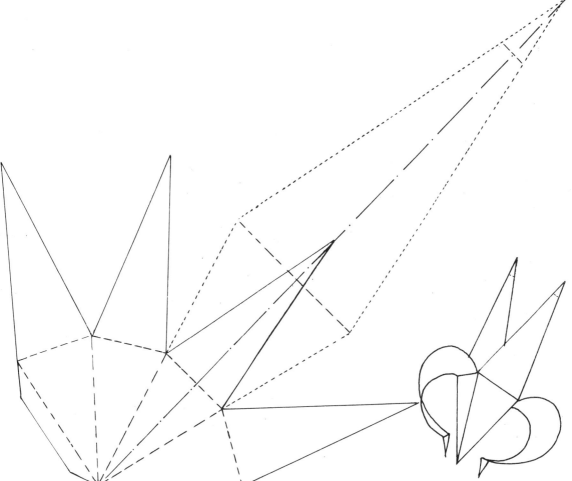

More cones

Each of these cones is made from a $5\frac{1}{2}$-inch square. Fold the paper diagonally to form a triangle and transfer the pattern onto the folded paper, with the dotted line along the folded edge. Cut it out, and smooth the paper so that the fold disappears. On the paper with the oblique slits, fold every second strip upward. Stick the edges of the cones together, and either stick on handles or thread ribbons through.

19

Christmas tree decorations

Make these decorations from duplicating or tracing paper, or some other paper of similar thickness. Transfer the shape onto a folded piece of paper, with the dotted line on the fold. Unfold the paper and lay three or four pieces under the one with the drawing on it; sew with your machine along the dotted line. Leave enough cotton thread at each end of the seam to fasten off securely, so that it does not come undone. Fold the sheets of paper around the seam, and cut out with sharp, pointed scissors, not too large. Separate the sheets of paper and spread them around the seam. With a piece of sewing-thread attached at the top, the decorations are ready to hang on the Christmas tree.

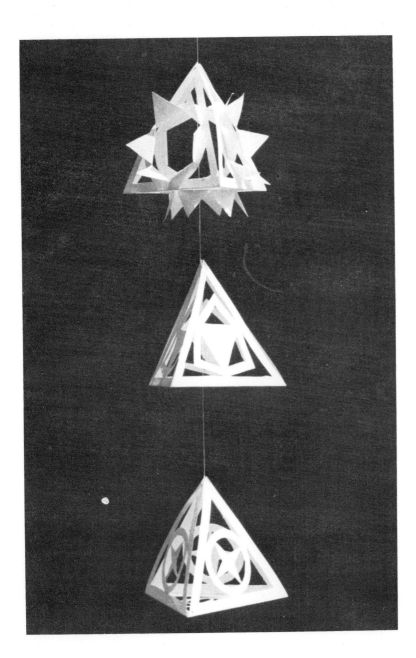

Decorations from triangles

If they are to look really well, these decorations must be made very accurately. It is best to construct the triangles with compasses, but the diagram can be traced straight off, provided this is done carefully. Draw the four triangles, and fold them together, over and under each other. Draw the design on the top one, and cut through all four layers. Unfold the triangles and draw a thread through the three points. Knot the thread, and the decoration is ready.

23

A three-dimensional star

Make this star from thin white cardboard or metal foil. First of all, construct a pattern to the given dimensions, following the heavy lines. Cut out the pattern. Now fold one of the squares along the dotted lines marked on fig. *a*. On a quarter of this square (fig. *b*) draw the lines, which are cut through all four layers. Unfold this square, and treat the other five squares in the same manner, keeping them joined by their corners. Bend the points on each square alternately to one side and the other. Fold the model into shape, making sharp creases along the dotted lines at the corners. Now paste the whole cube together, lapping the free corners over each other.

If you make two or three stars of different sizes and hang them inside each other, you will have a gay mobile.

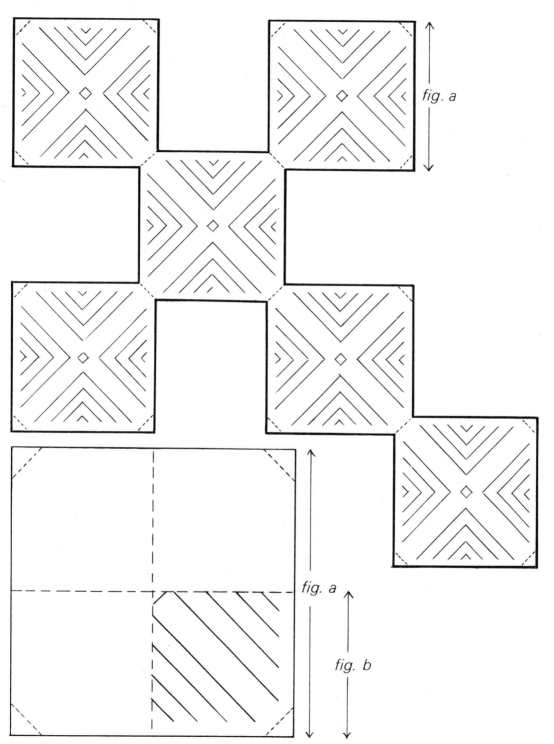

fig. a

fig. a

fig. b

Candlesticks

The candlesticks are made of white cardboard. Transfer the diagrams onto the cardboard, and cut them out with a thin, sharp knife, such as a craft knife. First, roll up the cardboard like a carpet, and stick it (fig. *a*). Now bend the roll into a ring (fig. *b*). Paste the front of one flap and the back of the other, so that the ring can be fastened together. Cut the base from a piece of strong cardboard, painted or covered with coloured paper. Both types of candlestick can be stuck onto the base either way up. NB You must stand the candle in a tin-foil holder (fig. *c*) before you set it in the candlestick. The dotted areas on the diagram show where to apply the paste.

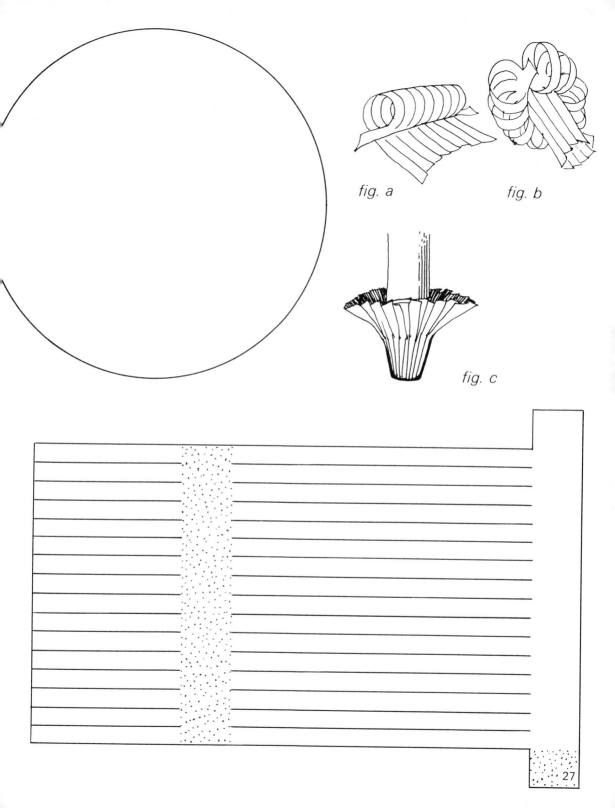

fig. a

fig. b

fig. c

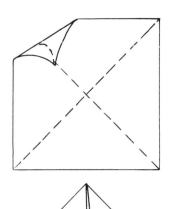

fig. a

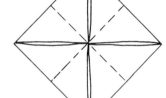

fig. b

fig. c

fig. d

fig. e

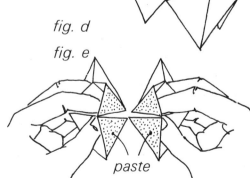

paste

14-pointed star

The star is made of six identically folded parts. Ordinary white notepaper is a suitable thickness. The method of folding the six parts is shown in figs *a*, *b* and *c*. The paper is 8 inches square. Fold it along the dotted lines, producing two diagonals. Fig. *b*—fold the four corners into the middle. Fig. *c*—reverse the paper and once again bring the four corners into the middle. Reverse the paper again. From this position, pull it outward to form the shape shown in fig. *d*. Now stick together the six units formed in this way (fig. *e*). Hang up the star by a piece of cotton thread. Further decoration can be added if you apply a little paste in each hollow and sprinkle some silver glitter powder.

Braided stars

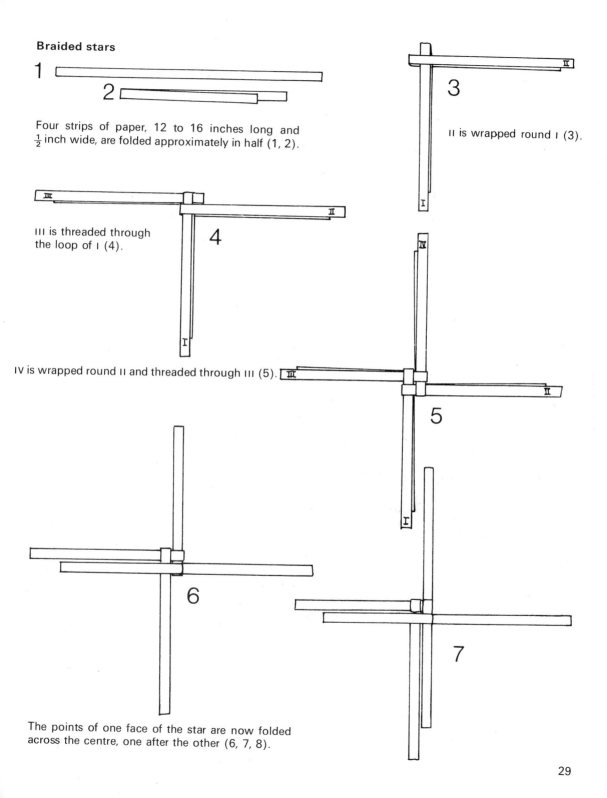

1

2

Four strips of paper, 12 to 16 inches long and $\frac{1}{2}$ inch wide, are folded approximately in half (1, 2).

3

II is wrapped round I (3).

III is threaded through the loop of I (4).

4

IV is wrapped round II and threaded through III (5).

5

6

7

The points of one face of the star are now folded across the centre, one after the other (6, 7, 8).

29

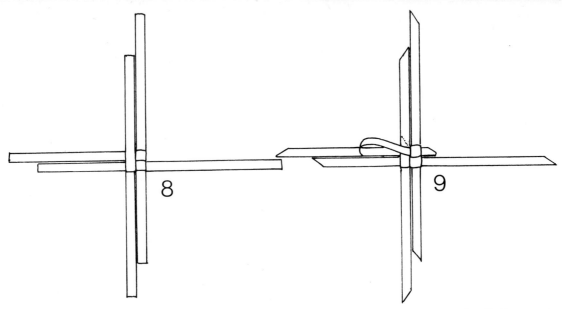

Finally, the braid or plait is secured by drawing the last strip through under the first (9).

Cut the end of each strip to a point. Fold one strip backward on the dotted line and

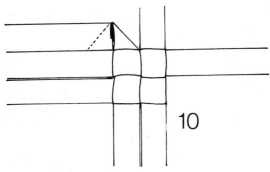

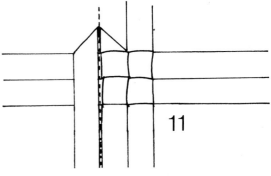

fold it forward on the dotted line (10). Fold it forward on the dotted line to make 12.
The little tag is bent gently backward, and the strip threaded through (13).

Repeat 10–13, turning the star through 90° each time, and repeat the process four times on the other side, to make 14.

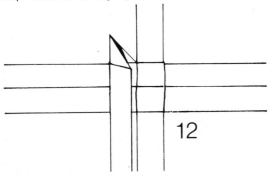

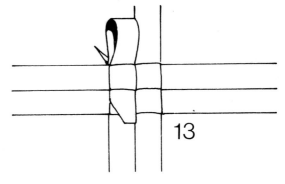

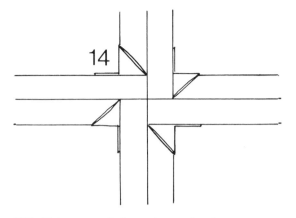

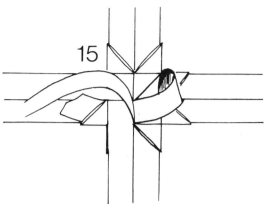

(15) Raise one of the strips, twist the adjacent one, as shown on the diagram, draw it through under the raised one, so that the end comes out in the middle of the little tag, pull the strip as far through as you can and a little cone will be formed (16).

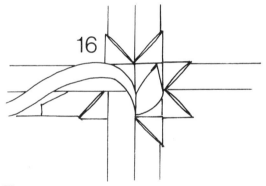

There are four cones like this on each face of the star (17). Cut off the excess strip along the dotted lines.

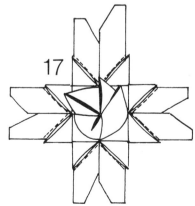

Make your stars into pretty things

The stars can be used to make many decorations to display attractively at all times of the year. Stick the stars together as shown in the diagram.

For the wreath, make 12 stars. Stick them together in a long strip; stand them up on edge and stick the ends together. Fasten a thread to every second star and gather the threads into a knot centrally above the wreath. With one thread rising from the knot, it is ready to hang up.

The long panel consists of stars stuck together in pairs and the pairs under each other. The length of the panel is up to you.

For the large star with the little ones beneath it, braid one star of strips 1 inch wide, and four little ones of strips $\frac{1}{2}$ inch wide. Hang them up as shown in the photograph.

The rectangular panel, displayed cornerwise, is simply 3×3 stars stuck together.

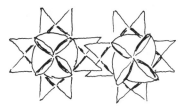

For Shrove Tuesday

The clowns and the cats are cut from paper folded accordion fashion. The dotted lines indicate the folds. Transfer the pattern onto the folded paper, cut it out, unfold it, and the clowns will stand up. They can each be coloured differently. The cats, of course, should be entirely black, but, otherwise, they are made in the same way. The barrel is made according to the diagram furthest to the right. Copy it onto paper, cut it out and make slits as marked. Paste the barrel together, sticking along the slits, too, to make the barrel shape. Stick a strip of paper, top and ·bottom, where the slits begin with a little black cat in the middle. For the spots, use some of the ·little circles from a paper-punch. The dotted areas show where to apply the paste.

34

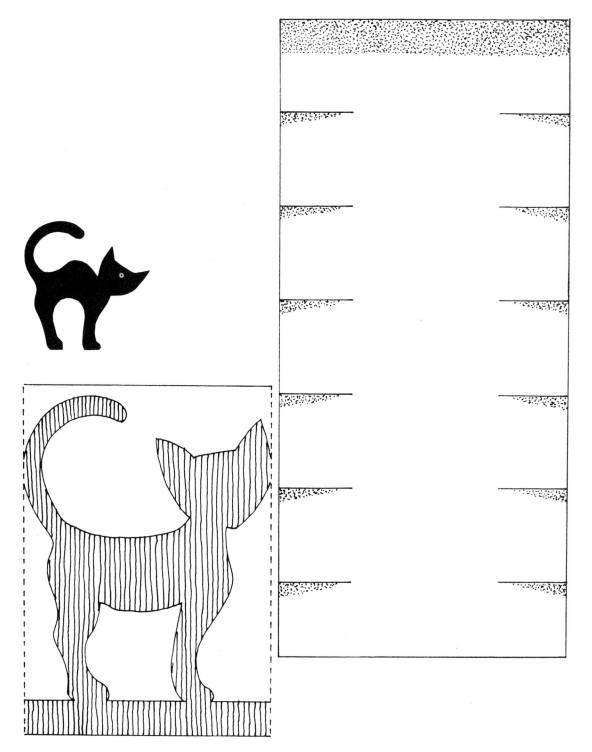

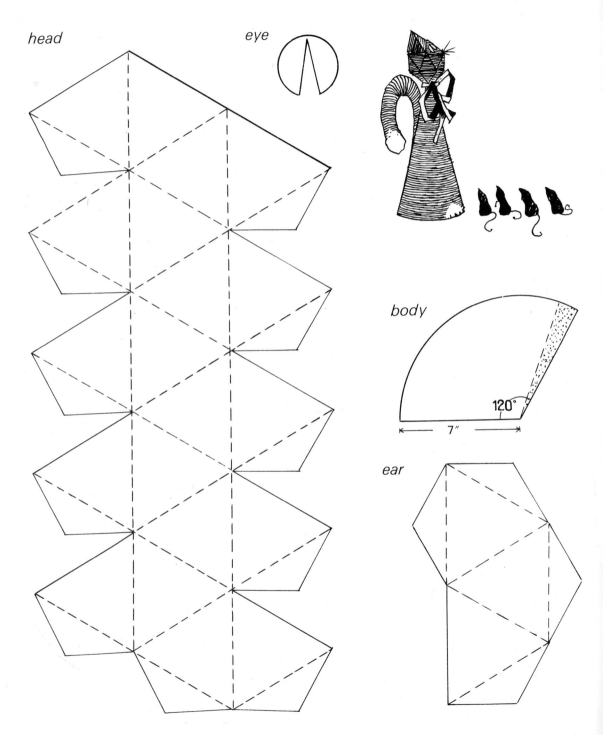

head

eye

body

120°

7"

ear

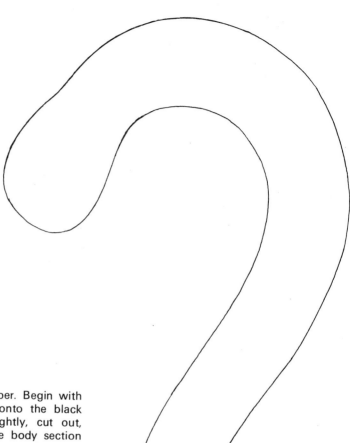

A cat for the table

The cat is made of mat black paper. Begin with the head. Transfer the diagram onto the black paper, score the dotted lines lightly, cut out, fold and stick together. Copy the body section to the given dimensions, cut it out and stick it together, holding it extra firmly with a piece of sticky tape inside. Now make a hole in the head (see fig. *a*) and fix it on top of the body, spreading the paste on the small flaps that stick out. Be very careful to fix the head on firmly, adding a piece of sticky tape round the neck. Draw the ears, cut them out and stick them together, after scoring along the fold lines. Now stick them onto the head; place them very carefully, as their position, in fact, gives the cat its expression. Stick on the eyes, cut in luminous green. The whiskers can be of sewing-cotton, but are even better made from fine copper wire (from an old radio loudspeaker, perhaps, or something similar). Stick them on with a little spot of glue at the centre of the muzzle. To make the tail, stick two pieces of black paper together so that it is black both sides. Fix it firmly to the body with two staples. Now the only thing left to do is to paint the paws and the tip of the tail white. A red bow round the cat's neck completes the figure.

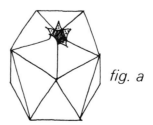

fig. a

A dog for the table

The figure is made of thin white card, but it would also look attractive made of brown paper. The dog is the same size as the cat, its body and head being made from the cat's diagram. Trace the muzzle, score, cut and fold it, then stick it firmly onto the head. The ears are curled a little at the edges before they are stuck on. In the picture, the top-knot and the tufts on paws and tail are made of long thin strips of paper, but they could also be made of cotton thread. The eyes are pink with a blue dot. The muzzle and the paws are picked out in black. The tail is fixed firmly to the body with two staples. Tie a pale blue bow round the dog's neck.

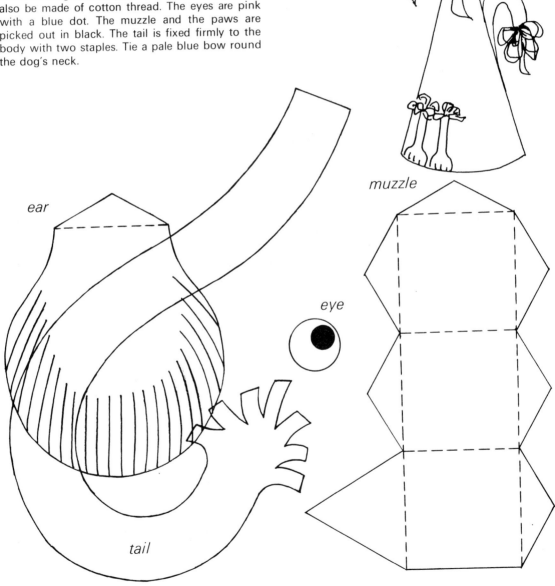

muzzle

ear

eye

tail

Easter cut-outs

Chicks and eggs. Cut out a strip, $\frac{3}{4} \times 16$ inches, and paste it into a ring. Trace the chicks onto yellow paper, preferably the kind that is self-coloured all through. Fold the paper, so that you can cut them two at a time. Cut out four coloured eggs. Stick eight chicks onto the band, two and two, with an egg between each pair (see photograph).

The egg-cups are simple. Trace the shape onto paper folded accordion fashion, so that the dotted lines lie on the folds. Cut through all the layers and unfold. Cut out brightly-coloured eggs and stick them to each side of the accordion.

The hen is cut from a folded piece of paper. Transfer the shape so that the lower dotted line lies on the fold. Cut the hen out. Draw the wings, cut them out and stick them on, bending them a little away from the body to look three-dimensional. Cut the head and comb from red paper and the beak from yellow paper; stick them on. Stick the hen together at the head, having first folded the centre section as shown on the small diagram.

16"

3/4"

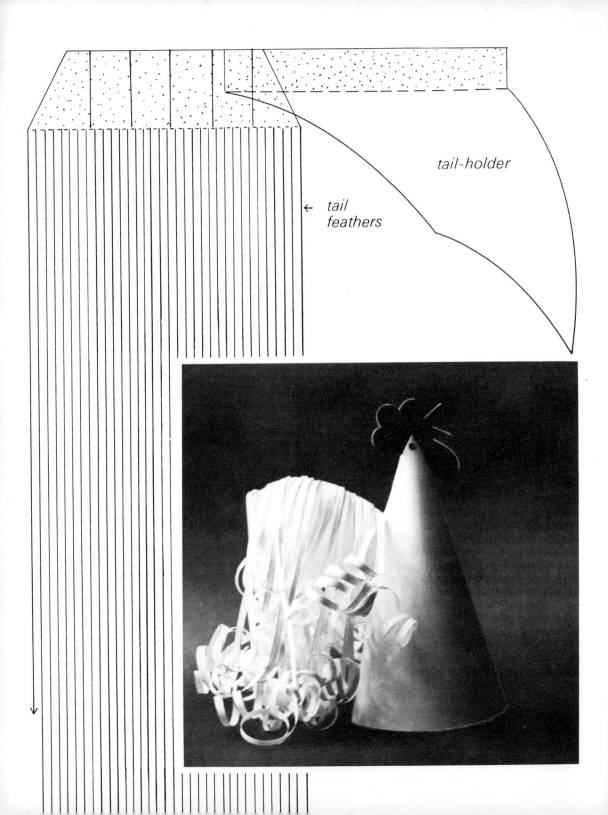

tail-holder

← *tail feathers*

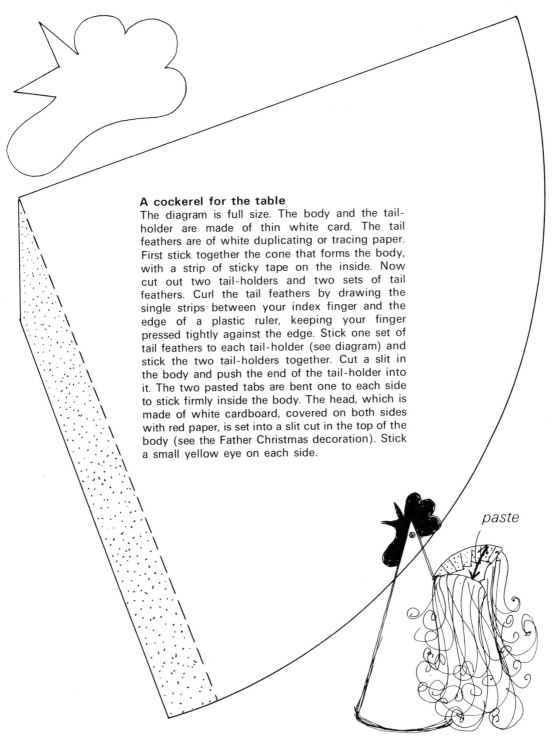

A cockerel for the table

The diagram is full size. The body and the tail-holder are made of thin white card. The tail feathers are of white duplicating or tracing paper. First stick together the cone that forms the body, with a strip of sticky tape on the inside. Now cut out two tail-holders and two sets of tail feathers. Curl the tail feathers by drawing the single strips between your index finger and the edge of a plastic ruler, keeping your finger pressed tightly against the edge. Stick one set of tail feathers to each tail-holder (see diagram) and stick the two tail-holders together. Cut a slit in the body and push the end of the tail-holder into it. The two pasted tabs are bent one to each side to stick firmly inside the body. The head, which is made of white cardboard, covered on both sides with red paper, is set into a slit cut in the top of the body (see the Father Christmas decoration). Stick a small yellow eye on each side.

paste

Animals for table decorations or murals

Transfer the shapes onto the actual paper that the animals are to be made from. For table decorations, stout paper, or, even better, thin cardboard, should be used. Fold the paper so that both sides of the animal are cut at once. The tortoise is the only creature in which the folded edge is used. It forms the top of the shell, and the animal is stuck together at head and tail. The patterns on the shell are also cut out and curved slightly. If you press the head and tail quite gently towards each other, the tortoise will stand.

The rocking-horse, the giraffe, the elephant, the camel and the dog are pasted together at the head and half way down the body (the dotted line on the camel gives an indication of how far) so that the legs can be bent outwards from each other and the creatures can stand. The elephant's ears are cut out separately and stuck on with a line of paste at the top. The swans are cut out with the folded edge against the lower dotted line, and are stuck together only at head and neck. The central section that they stand on is folded as for the hen. The water-lily is made of three sections: the large flower, the small flower that is stuck on top of it and finally, the yellow centre patch. Bend all the petals upwards and it is ready.

The diagrams can also be used for murals, with one or more of the same animal, or one large and one small of each to make a mother with young.

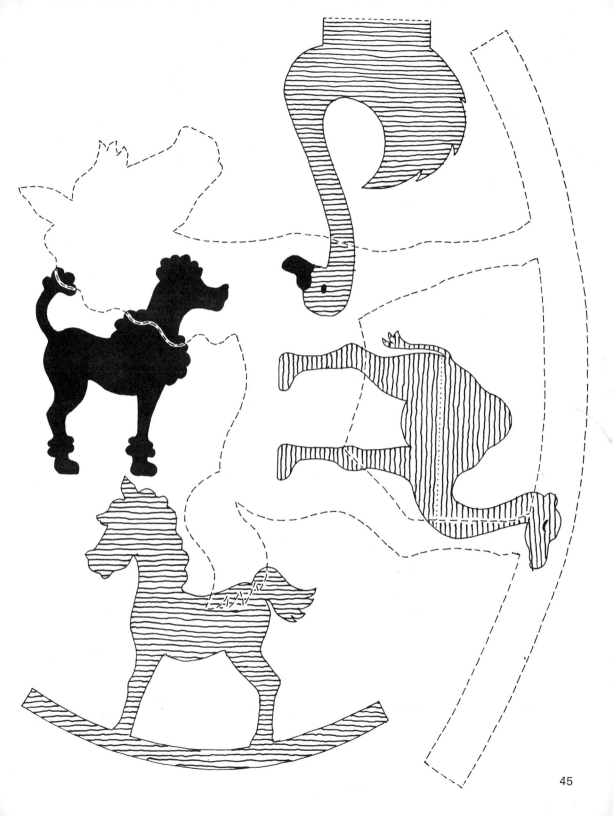

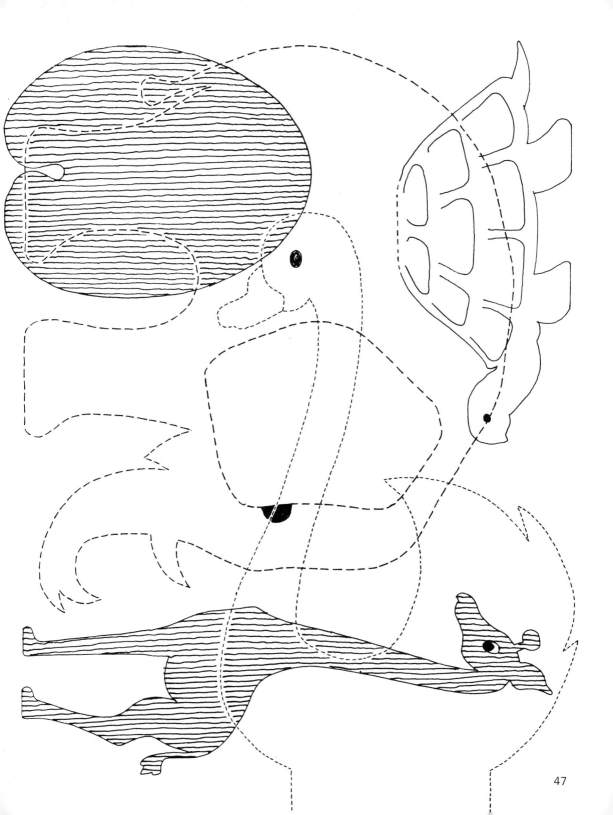

47

Table decorations

Fold the paper, accordion fashion, four or five times—any more would make it too thick to cut. Transfer the patterns onto the folded paper so that the dotted lines lie on the folds. Cut out and unfold. If you need a longer strip, cut out another batch and stick them together. Faces and dresses painted on the dolls look gay. The elephant can wear a decorative mat. These figures can be used to decorate invitation cards and the like.

49

Peacock

This ornamental peacock is not so difficult to make as it looks. Transfer the diagram onto folded paper so that the dotted line lies on the fold. Cut out the body and tail. On the body, make slits for the beak and the feathers. Unfold the paper and bend them forwards. Bend the body round and fix it with paste. As you cut out the tail, clip the oblique slits and heart on the fold. Now fold along the dotted line at the place where the next heart is to be; cut out the heart, make the oblique slits and unfold. Make a fold for the next heart, and so on, until all four hearts are cut. Now unfold the whole tail. On each of the seven rows, every second one of the little points is folded upwards. Give the tail a dab of paste at the base

and clip it together to make it shapely. Stick on a small paper strip, so that the tail is prettily curved and will stand up. The tailpiece of the peacock's body is stuck through a slit in the big tail. Bend it upwards and the bird is complete. This makes a table decoration or a menu-card. For this, simply leave the centre line of slits uncut, so that the plain area can be written on.

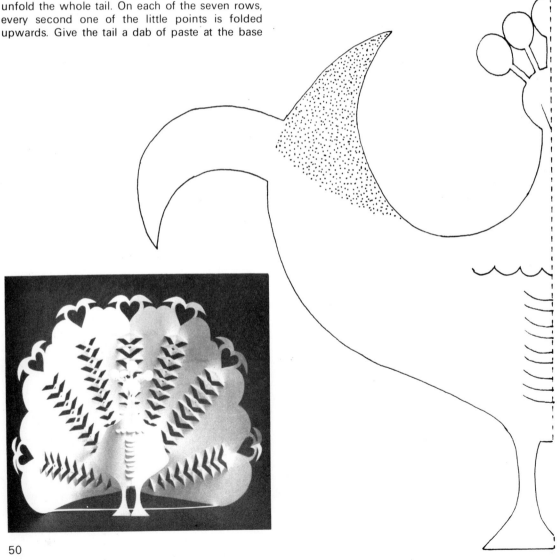

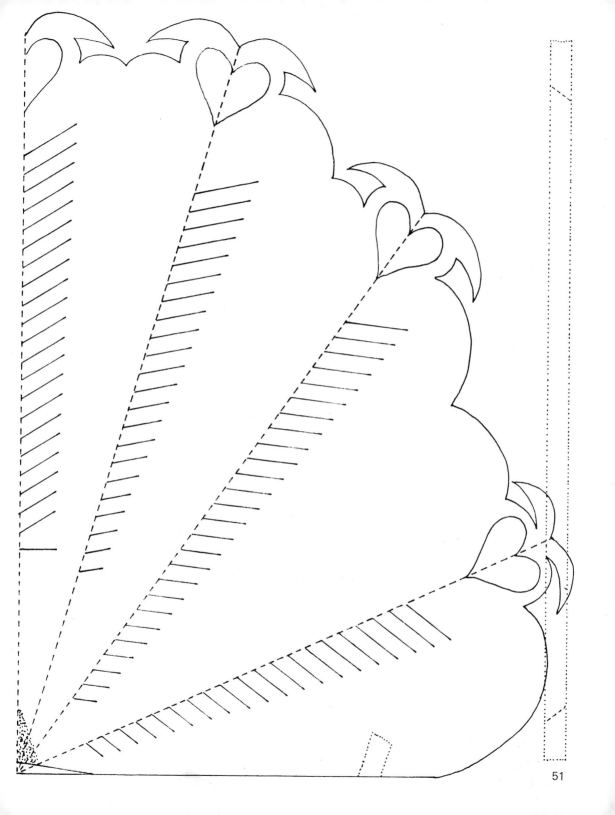

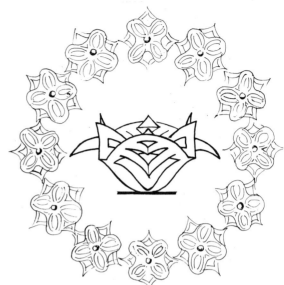

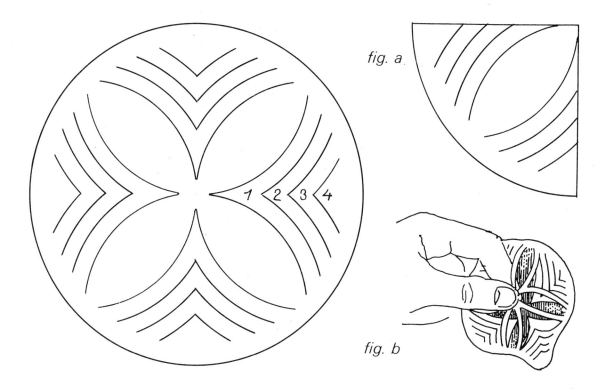

fig. a

fig. b

A string of lotus blossoms

Each flower is made of a single piece of paper. Draw a circle with radius of the size shown, cut it out and fold it twice at right angles (fig. *a*). Draw the pattern of thin lines on this quarter-circle. Cut along the lines through all four layers at once. All the 1-points (see fig. *b*) are pasted, one above the other, the 2-points are folded to the opposite side, the 3-points remain where they are and the 4-points are folded the opposite way to the 2-points. Each individual flower is threaded onto the string with a needle. Start with a knot in the thread, draw one flower on and make a knot where the next flower is to rest.

For table decorations

Cut the flowers from coloured paper to match your cloth. Stick each one onto a small piece of cardboard (see the drawing inside the wreath). Arrange the paper flowers on the table in a long row or in a circle.

A frame for pin-up pictures

First stick the picture to be framed onto a square or circular piece of cardboard; arrange the flowers round it so that their centres coincide with the edge of the picture. When these flowers are used for a table decoration or for a frame, a small bead should be fixed firmly at the place where the flower itself is stuck together.

Fish on a line

The diagrams are full size. The fish are made from white cardboard, but would also be eye-catching made from metal foil. Transfer the shapes onto cardboard and cut them out. The dotted lines are the fold lines for the scales. Fold the scales outward on each side to give a three-dimensional effect. Assemble the fish on a fine thread, drawn through the points indicated on the bodies. Make a knot in the thread between each pair of fish, to keep them a suitable distance apart (about an inch).

Hanging birds

These birds are quick and easy to make. Trace the bird in the ring onto cardboard and cut it out. Draw the ring either from the diagram or with compasses. Cut it out and fix the bird firmly by the slits above and below. Hang it up by sewing-cotton.

Transfer the flying bird—two body pieces and two wings—onto cardboard and cut it out. Cut the slits for the wings and stick them on, one wing to each body piece, as the body is stuck together afterwards. Paste only as far as the dotted line, as the two tail sections are spread outward from each other. Hang the bird by a thread drawn through the dot above the wing-slit.

Bird of Paradise

The diagram is full size. The bird is made of ordinary white drawing-paper. Transfer the diagram onto the paper and cut it out. Curl the head and neck feathers in opposite directions, drawing the individual strips between your index finger and the edge of a plastic ruler (see the diagram). Curl the tail feathers lightly. Stick the wings together so that they lap over each other slightly.

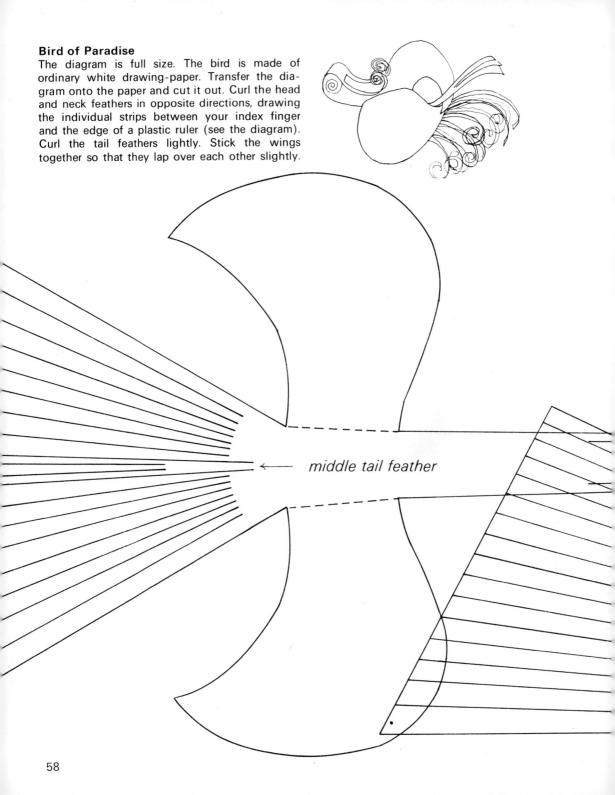

← *middle tail feather*

Draw the middle tail feather up over the wings. Hang the bird up from a long piece of sewing-cotton fastened by a knot at the black dot on each wing.

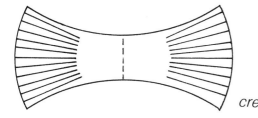

crest

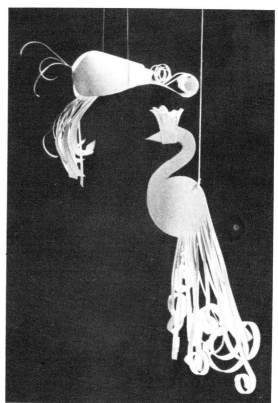

Hanging peacock

The diagram is full size. Transfer the diagram onto white cardboard and cut it out. Curl the tail feathers alternately one way and the other. Draw the crest and cut it out. Curl the feathers so that each set bends outwards when it is folded and stuck onto the head. The dotted lines show the location. Hang the peacock up on a thread drawn through the little black dot on its back.

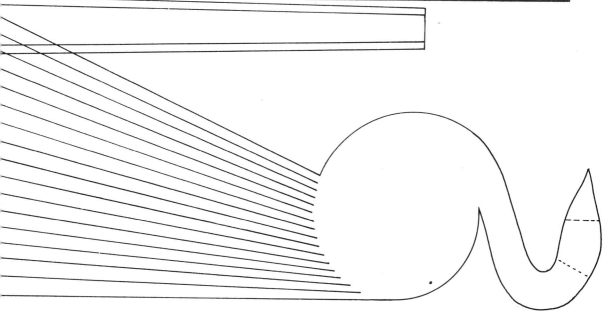

wing support

A bird with punched patterns

The diagram is full size. Trace the bird's body onto a piece of thin white cardboard, cut it out and make the holes with a paper-punch. Cut five wing feathers, and punch holes to match in each of them. Lay the five feathers on top of each other and stick a needle through the central hole of all five at once. Draw the needle out again. Thread the feathers through the wing slit in the bird's body, and put a little paste on each feather round the needle hole. Arrange the feathers on top of each other and stick the needle through again.

Spread the feathers into two wing-fans (see diagram). The paste must not dry until this point in the process. Now adjust the position of the wings so that the needle hole is at the place where the body and wings meet. To hold the wings in place, stick a small supporting piece on each side of the body under the wings (see the dotted lines on the diagram). From the little hole in the back, hang the bird up on sewing-cotton threaded through two holes in the tail for support.

Butterfly fantasy

Use brightly-coloured paper, not too heavy. Transfer the pattern onto folded paper, with the broken line on the fold. Cut out the butterfly, unfold it and bend its wings gently upwards. Now it is ready to be stuck onto a wall panel (see photograph), an invitation card, a napkin ring made of a cardboard tube from a kitchen-roll, or, quite simply, onto a circle of card to form a table decoration.

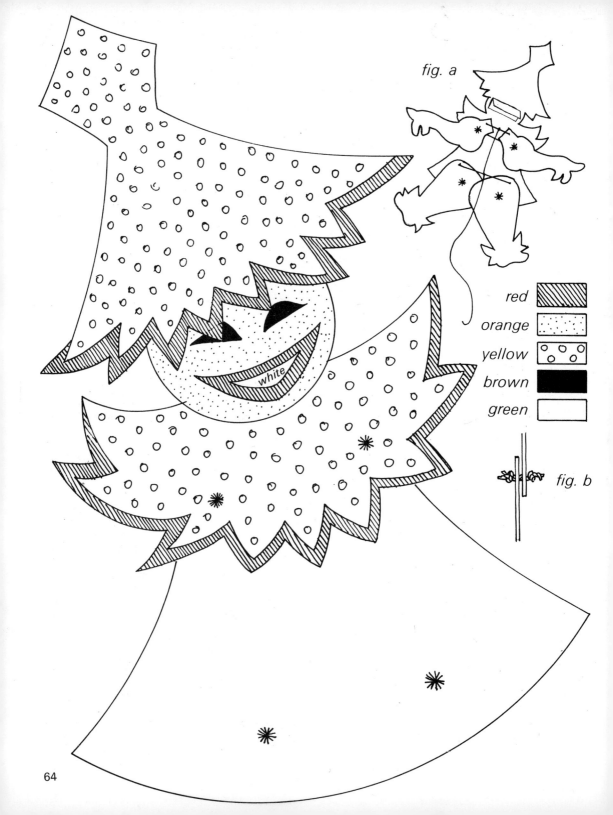

fig. a

red

orange

yellow

brown

green

white

fig. b

64

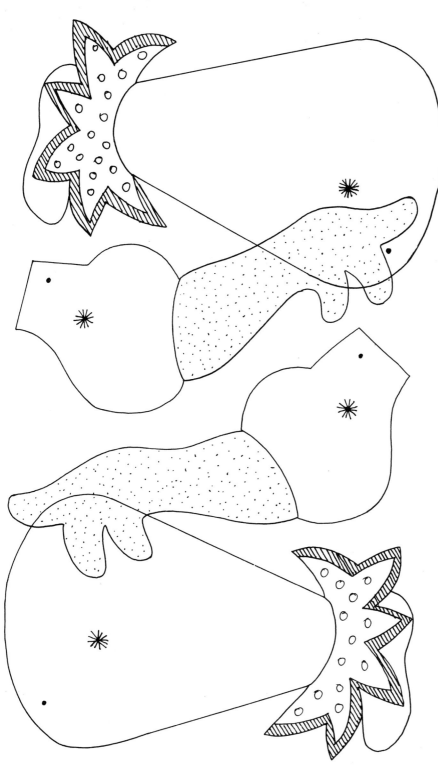

Jumping Jill

Trace the diagram onto coloured paper, cut it out and paste it onto cardboard. Now cut out the completed arms, legs and body. Fig. *a* indicates the placing of the arms and legs on the body, through the stars.

Using a length of twine, make a knot on each side of the two pieces of cardcoard (see fig. *b*). The small black dots on arms and legs show where the working string is to be fixed (see fig. *a*). Fix a folded piece of cardboard behind the head to stop the arms and legs from swinging right round and getting stuck.

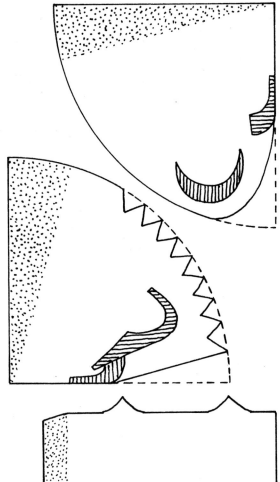

The Three Kings

The diagram is full size. Materials needed: brightly-coloured paper, three cocktail sticks and three Styrofoam balls, getting on for 1 inch in diameter. All the cone-shapes are semicircles, pasted together up the back. Begin with the body, either drawing it out with compasses or tracing it from the diagram. Stick it together and decorate it. The upper cone is cut out, folded in half and clipped to shape in the front, as the illustration shows. Paste it together at the back. Stick on the hands and the borders. Push a cocktail stick up through the tips of the two cones, and top it with a Styrofoam ball (see the small diagram). Two of the Styrofoam balls should be coloured pink, the other black. Cut out the beard from black paper and stick it on. The crowns are cut from gold foil. Stick the ends together and place the crowns on top.

66

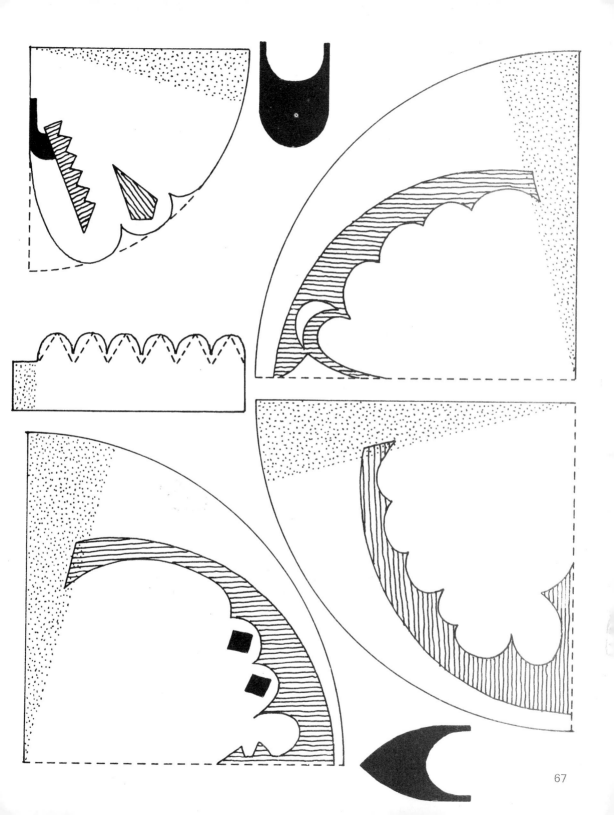

67

Plaited hearts

Four strips of red gloss paper, 18–20 inches long and 1 inch wide, are folded together at the centre, two of them showing their white sides and two of them their red sides. Number each strip at both ends and on both sides; the two white strips are numbered respectively 1 and 2, and the red ones 3 and 4.

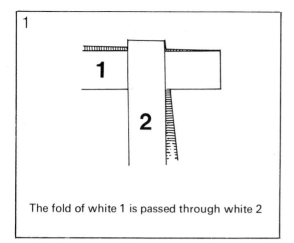

1

The fold of white 1 is passed through white 2

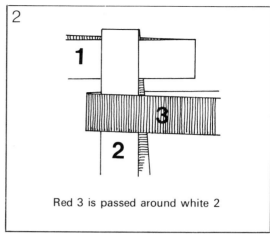

2

Red 3 is passed around white 2

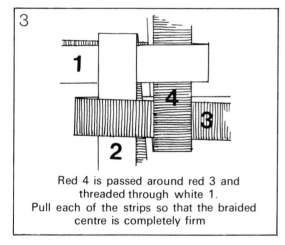

3

Red 4 is passed around red 3 and threaded through white 1.
Pull each of the strips so that the braided centre is completely firm

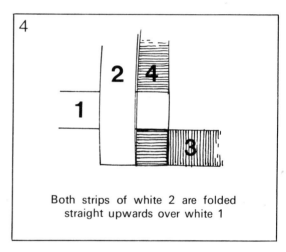

4

Both strips of white 2 are folded straight upwards over white 1

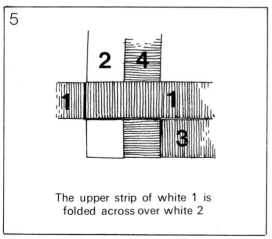

5

The upper strip of white 1 is folded across over white 2

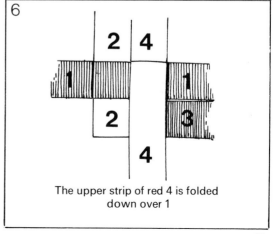

6

The upper strip of red 4 is folded down over 1

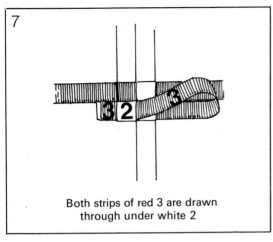

7

Both strips of red 3 are drawn through under white 2

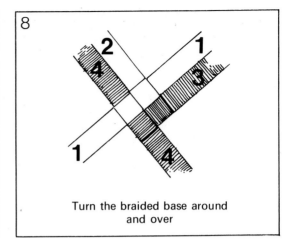

8

Turn the braided base around and over

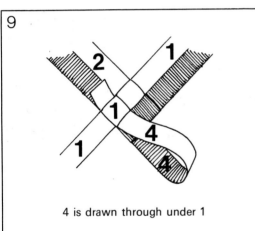

9

4 is drawn through under 1

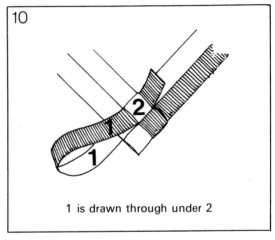

10

1 is drawn through under 2

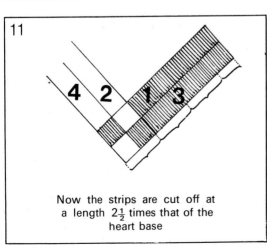

11

Now the strips are cut off at a length $2\frac{1}{2}$ times that of the heart base

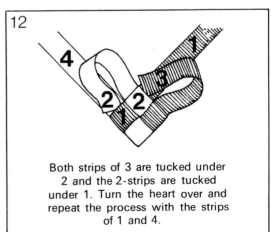

12

Both strips of 3 are tucked under 2 and the 2-strips are tucked under 1. Turn the heart over and repeat the process with the strips of 1 and 4.

A wreath of hearts

The wreath is made of 10 hearts (strips 18 inches long by 1 inch wide). When the 10 hearts have been braided, they are assembled as shown in fig. *m*. The front heart-loop to the left is un-

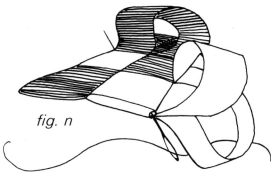

fig. n

fig. m

fastened and threaded downwards through the adjoining heart's front right loop, and so back into its place.

When all 10 hearts have been braided into a circle, they can be kept firmly together by a thread drawn through the whole wreath (fig. *n*).

The needle is pushed in through the little hole in the corner of the chequered square, and comes out of the corresponding hole on the opposite side.

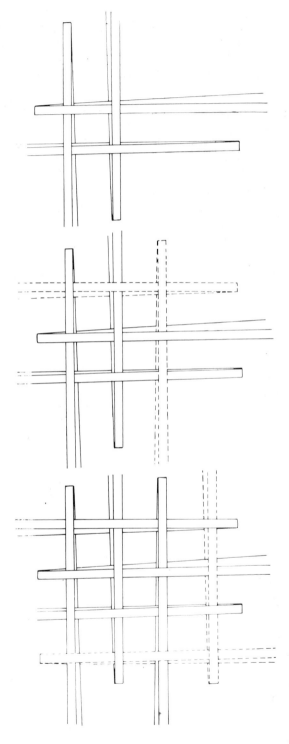

Plaited decoration

Eight paper strips, about $\frac{1}{4}$ inch wide and 14 inches long, are folded at the centre and braided into a square base, as shown in figs *a, b, c*. It is easiest to braid with strips lying on the table. The four first strips are plaited as in fig. *a*. The next two strips are braided in as shown by the broken lines in fig. *b*. The last two strips are braided in as shown by the broken lines in fig. *c*. Now pull the eight strips together so that the braided base is completely firm. Innumerable variations are now possible on this braided base, by bending the strips and tucking them down at various points in the square.

Begin by cutting the ends of each strip to a point.

The upper layer of one strip is curved over and tucked into the base (fig. 1)—repeat at the other three corners (fig. 2). The base is turned over and the process repeated, mirror-wise (fig. 3).

The upper layer of each of the four remaining double strips is tucked into the base as shown in fig. 4.

This is done on each side of the base. Fig. 5 shows the reverse side of fig. 4. Fig. 6 shows what the star looks like from the side.

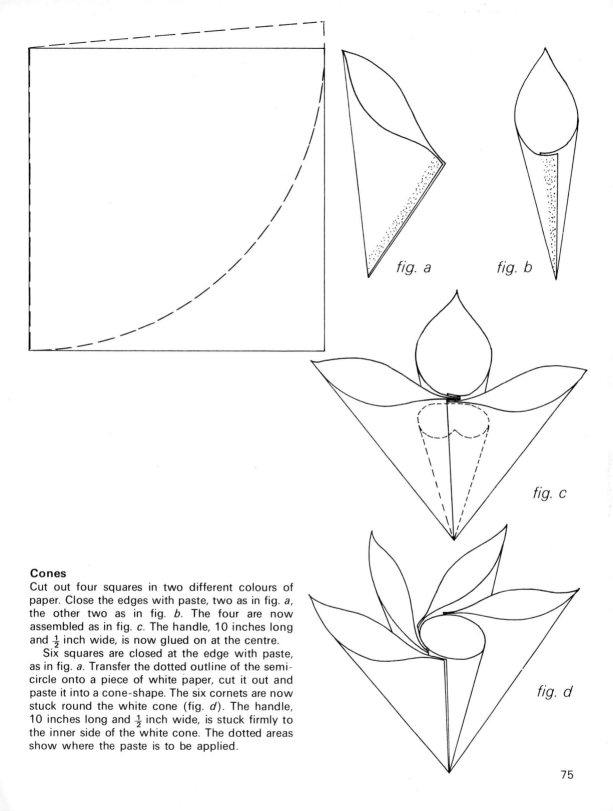

fig. a

fig. b

fig. c

fig. d

Cones

Cut out four squares in two different colours of paper. Close the edges with paste, two as in fig. *a*, the other two as in fig. *b*. The four are now assembled as in fig. *c*. The handle, 10 inches long and $\frac{1}{2}$ inch wide, is now glued on at the centre.

Six squares are closed at the edge with paste, as in fig. *a*. Transfer the dotted outline of the semi-circle onto a piece of white paper, cut it out and paste it into a cone-shape. The six cornets are now stuck round the white cone (fig. *d*). The handle, 10 inches long and $\frac{1}{2}$ inch wide, is stuck firmly to the inner side of the white cone. The dotted areas show where the paste is to be applied.

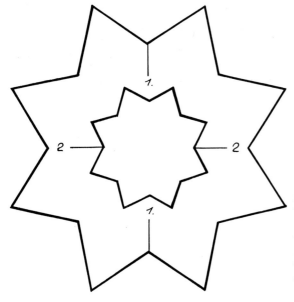

fig. a

Star

The star is made of strong white cardboard. The heavy lines on the diagram indicate the shape: cut two. Snip both no. 1 slits in the first shape, both no. 2 slits in the second. Now bend the star with the 1-slits so that it can be pushed through the central hole in the other star (fig. *a*). The two pairs of slits, 1 and 2, are now opposite each other, and are slotted together. Fix a short hanging thread at the place where the two slits meet.

Bead orange

Cut six hollow discs from orange, gold or silver paper. Fold them along the broken line and stick five of them together (fig. *b*). Thread a bead onto cotton thread and secure it with a knot. Arrange the bead so that it hangs in the space between the discs, with the thread lying up along the line of the fold. Stick the last disc in place and tie one more knot over all.

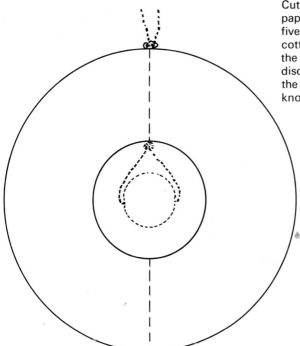

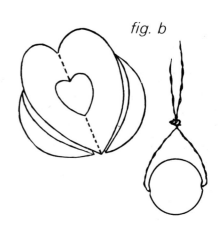

fig. b

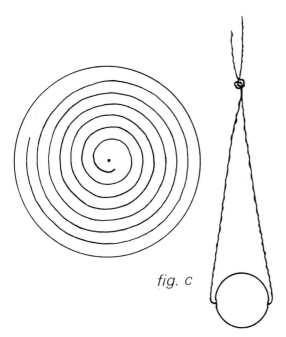

fig. c

Bead bell

The bell is made of a piece of stout white paper and an orange bead. Cut out a spiral. Thread the bead and tie a knot above it (fig. c). With a needle, draw the thread through the top of the spiral; knot the thread again, and use the remainder of it to hang the bell up.

Bead sun

From orange and red paper, cut out six strips: two of 6 inches length, two of 8 inches and two of 10 inches, all $\frac{1}{2}$ inch wide. Now stick each pair together, as shown in fig. d. Thread the bead and make a knot above it. With a needle, draw the thread through the strips of the smallest 'sun' at the point where they are joined. Tie another knot and tuck the smallest 'sun' into the middle-sized one. Tie another knot and tuck both 'suns' into the biggest one. Tie another knot and use the rest of the thread to hang up the completed 'sun'.

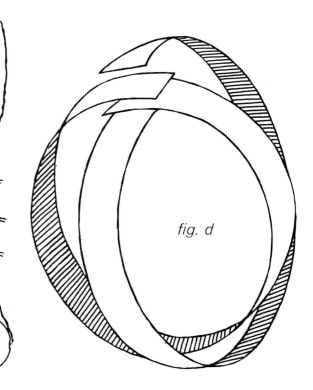

fig. d

77

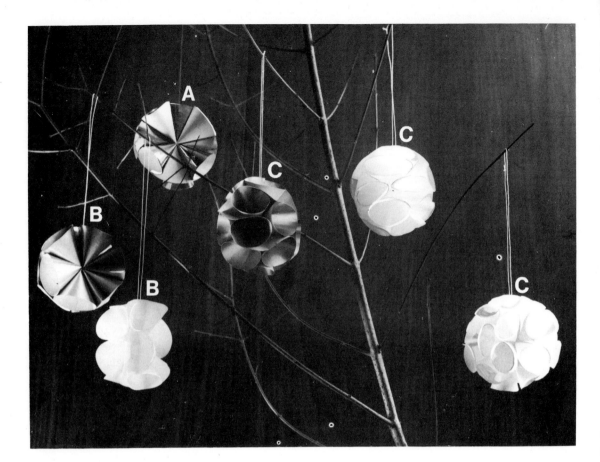

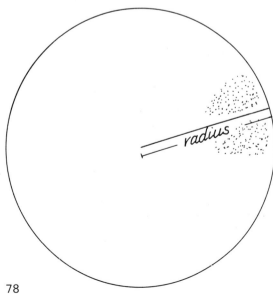

radius

Christmas tree decorations
Only one shape is used in the making of these decorations but it is assembled in different combinations and made from various kinds of paper. (The dotted areas show where to apply the paste.)

A.
Cut out six circles of gold paper. On four of them cut along one radius; shape and stick each one separately, as shown in fig. *a*, two of them with the white side outwards and two with the gold side outwards. Lay the remaining two circles, gold side up, on the table, and stick two of the rolled circles onto each. Now stick the base-circles together with the hanging thread firmly between them.

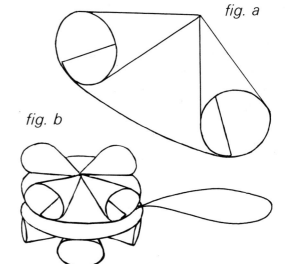

fig. a

fig. b

B.
Cut out six circles from gold, silver or tissue paper; cut each one along the radius; shape and stick them separately, as in fig. *c*. Cut out two of a slightly smaller circle and stick three of the double cones onto each small circle (fig. *d*). The two matching halves are now stuck together with the hanging thread firmly between them.

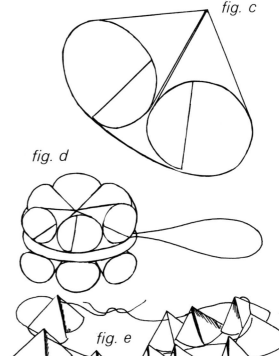

fig. c

fig. d

fig. e

C.
Cut out 10 circles of gold, silver or tissue paper. Cut each along one radius; shape and stick them separately, as in fig. *c*. Thread all 10 double cones onto a cord and knot the two ends together as tightly as possible without damaging them. Use the cord for hanging the decoration.

Easter hens and cockerels

The diagrams are full size for tracing off. Transfer the shapes onto cardboard, cut them out and decorate as in the diagrams. The cockerel and hen with hearts on them should be in gay colours. The feet are semicircles, rolled and stuck to make cones, with slits from the top extending barely halfway down each side. The two slits must be of equal length, or the figures will stand crookedly.

foot for large hen and cockerel

foot for small cockerel and hen

foot for chick

81

83

Parrot and parakeet

The diagram is full size. The ring is used for both birds and is cut from strong cardboard. First, the outline of the parrot is transferred onto cardboard and cut out. Next, the various parts are transferred onto coloured paper. You might, for instance, have wings, body and tail in shades of blue. Cut out the various parts and stick them on. The beak and claws are yellow and the eye-surrounds grey.

The bird with the closed eyes: Transfer the shapes of the body and the two wings onto brightly-coloured card and cut them out. Draw the eye and beak on both sides and stick the wings on. Cut the tail-feathers from tissue paper, preferably in two colours, such as orange and yellow. Stick five feathers above each other on each side of the tail-point of the body. When the bird has been fixed into the ring, it is ready to hang up.

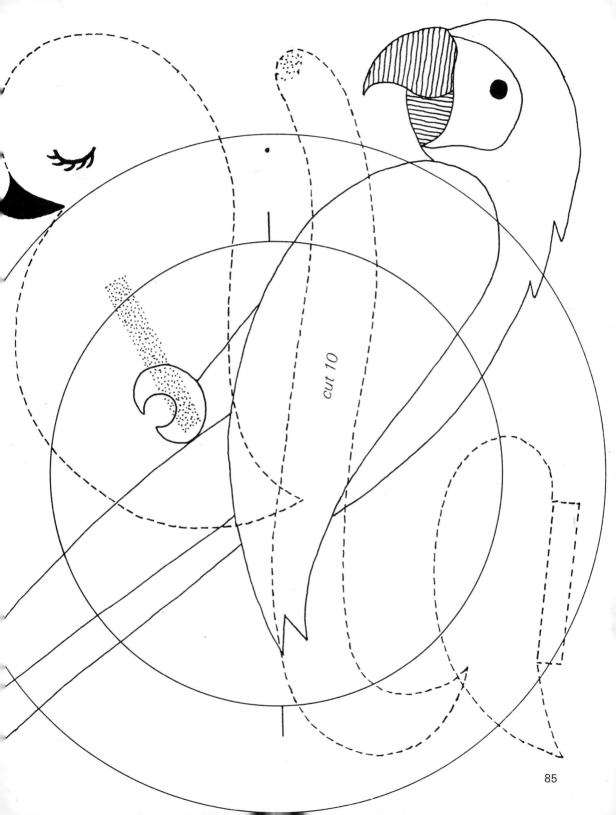

cut 10

Mother owl and her chicks

The diagram is full size. The material is thin card-board. Transfer the diagram onto the cardboard and cut it out. The oval that the mother owl is sitting in should not be folded; you can draw the complete oval by first of all tracing one side, then reversing the tracing paper so that the broken lines lie above each other, and then drawing the other side. Slit the birds' feathers with a sharp knife and fold along the dotted lines, alternately to one side and the other. The beak and the feet must face the same way. Cut out the eye circles; draw on the eyes, or cut them from paper and stick them on. The completed eye-circles are stuck onto the dotted areas. Hang the mother owl in the oval, with two chicks on each branch. The chicks do not need to hang from a thread, but can be made to perch on the ends of the branches, as in the photograph.

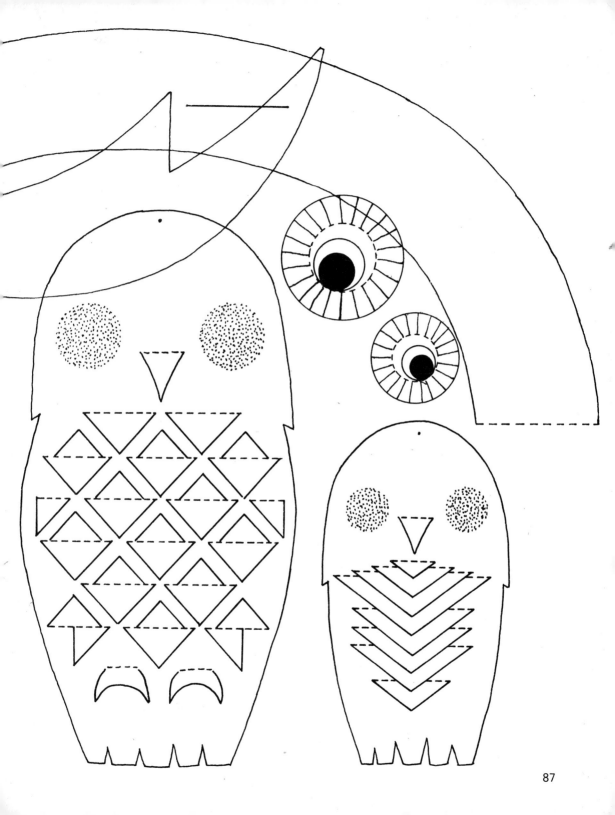

Hovering bird

The diagram is full size. Transfer both sides of the shape onto paper *without* folding along the dotted line, except at the head end as far as the mark. Cut out the bird and bend it so that the wings lie one above the other. Stick the two sides of the head and, with a thin strip of paste, secure the fold from the neck out onto the wing. When this is dry, bend the wings away from each other and downwards, securing them with a small spot of paste at the edge nearest the neck (see diagram). The bird is suspended from three strings, fastened at the points marked by the crosses. The strings are gathered in a knot, from which one extends to hang the bird up by.

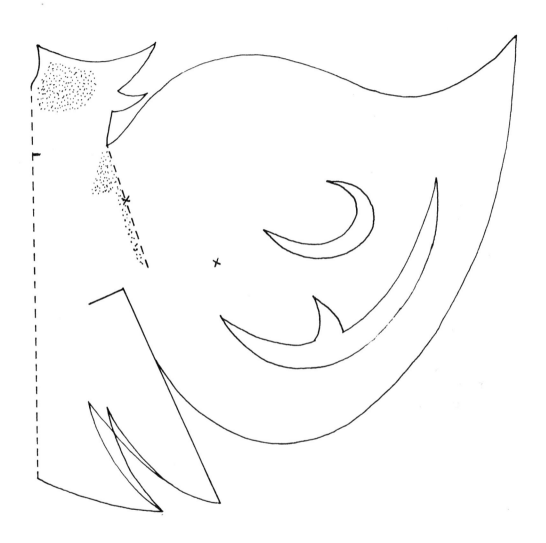

Hearts

The diagram is full size. For the heart mobile, draw a circle on cardboard round a large dessert plate. Cut it out and stick silver foil on one side, or fold the foil over the edges so that it lies smooth. The hearts are stuck together in pairs, orange and red, with the thread between them. Leave $1-1\frac{1}{2}$ inches between each. Eight sets of threaded hearts are set round the cardboard disc, about an inch from the edge. The silver paper is on the under side. The four hanging strings are joined in a knot, from which one string extends.

A globe of hearts. Cut six circles of thin cardboard and fold them down the centre. Stick them so that all the folds meet in the middle and cut the slits to hold the hearts. These are cut from red paper, folded into six. Draw a heart on the top layer, having the broken lines on the folds. Leave a small tab on the last heart, so that the circle can be stuck together.

The garland of hearts is cut from a circle of paper folded four times. Draw half a heart touching both the folds, or fold the paper three times only and draw a complete heart. NB the sides of the hearts must be touching. Use this as a table decoration, or as trimming for a card.

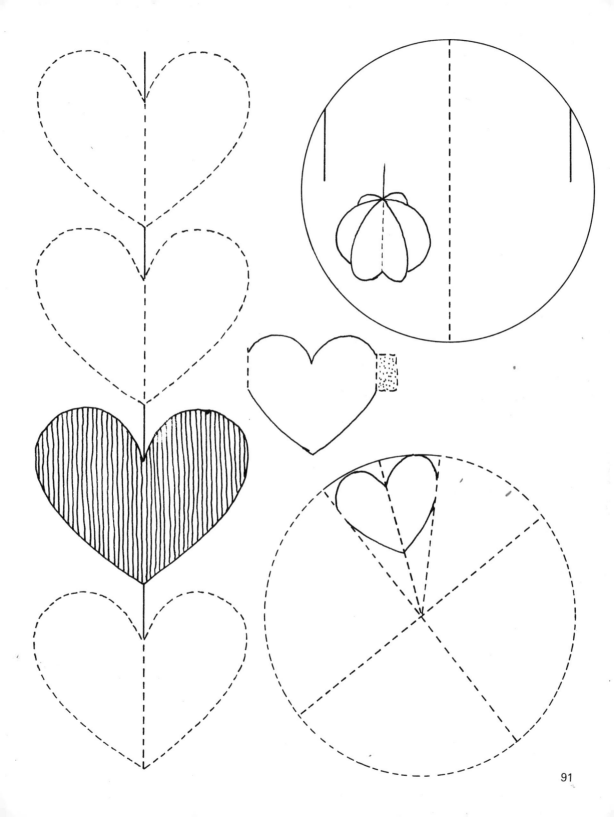

A mobile from cardboard tubes

The mobile is made from two sizes of cardboard tubes. You can use the inside tubes from kitchen paper or toilet rolls, or ask at the stationer's, when you buy paper, to have it packed in a cardboard tube. The tubes are cut into rings $\frac{1}{2}$ inch deep. Cut some long strips of paper, gold and white, in the same width. In the picture, the large rings are covered on the outside with gold paper and on the inside with white. The small rings are decorated the reverse way.

Draw the six dotted lines on a sheet of paper, and set a ring exactly over the place where all the lines meet. Then arrange the other rings so that they touch the first one, but lie between the dotted lines. Use the plan to arrange large rings of equal size symmetrically. The dotted circles show how to arrange smaller rings.

When the rings are arranged in the pattern you have chosen, make a small mark at each of the points where they touch, and put a dot of paste there. Deal with one ring at a time and fix it to the others. When all the rings are stuck together, hold them firm with clothes-pegs while the paste dries. It must be completely dry before the beads are added.

Using a needle and strong thread, start with a knotted end. Thread on a little circle of cardboard and then the bead. Make a knot in the thread so that it will hang the right length, draw it through where the bead is to hang, tie another knot and clip the thread off (see diagram).

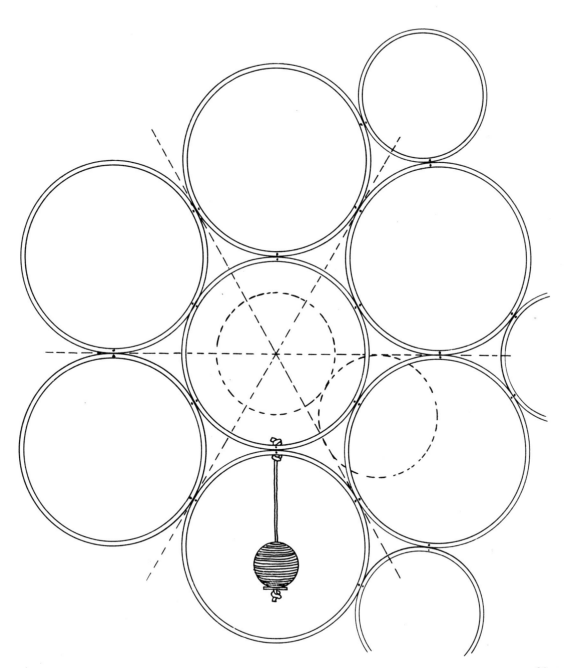

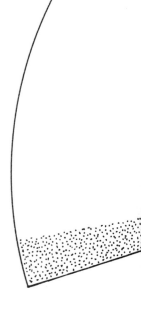

Bird-table house

The diagram is full size. Transfer the various sections onto thin cardboard and cut them out. Choose for yourself how many birds to have in and on the house. The small circle is the floor of the house. Push four thin sticks through the four black dots and down into four Styrofoam balls, which should be about $\frac{1}{2}$ inch in diameter. Paste together the straight sides cut from the large circle; push the sticks through it about $\frac{1}{2}$ inch from the edge and up into the Styrofoam balls.

You may choose what length you have the sticks. Assemble the parts of the birds. The feeding birds have their tails folded together round their bodies and stuck on at the dotted area. On the flying bird, the wings are bent a little upward. The bird table can be used for a table decoration, or hung from a string drawn through the tip of the roof. If the bird table is to be hung up, the birds should be stuck on first, making sure that the whole model balances properly.

Table decorations or toys

All diagrams are full size. Transfer the horse onto a sheet of thin cardboard, folded so that both sides are cut at once; stick it together at the head and tail, and down the body as far as the dotted line. Bend the legs outwards, so that the horse will stand up. Trace the mane, tail and saddle onto coloured paper, and cut them out double, to allow for both sides; stick them on; draw the horse's eyes.

Trace the doll's pram onto thin coloured cardboard and cut it out. Remember to cut a long central strip, 2×8 inches. Fold each of the long sides of this strip towards you, $\frac{1}{4}$ inch from the edge, and cut small snips from this border, so that the curve of the pram's sides can be followed more accurately, when you assemble the pram. Stick on the four wheels and the handle.

The princess, the cowboy and the Indians are all made in a similar way. Transfer the shapes onto a folded piece of thin cardboard, so that the lower broken line lies on the folded edge. Next, trace the individual parts onto coloured paper; most of them are alike, front and back, and can be cut out double. The back sections of those parts where front and back differ are drawn with broken lines. Stick the various pieces onto the body and draw the eyes and mouth. The feathers on the Indian's head-dress are drawn as shown. Each figure is stuck together at the head, neck and arms. The central section, on which the figures stand, is folded as shown in the diagram. The Indian's feather head-dress is bent down over his back, so that only the three central feathers can be seen from the front. The brim of the cowboy's hat is turned up slightly, before being slotted on.

Transfer the canoe onto a piece of thin cardboard, folded, so that the lower broken line lies on the fold. Cut it out. Fold the centre section, as for the princess, stick the canoe together at the ends and add the decoration. Transfer the Indian boy onto cardboard; remember to cut two. The two arms and the paddle for each one are drawn separately and stuck on, as are the hair, browband and feather. Both figures are stuck firmly to the floor of the canoe. Transfer the tent onto thin cardboard, cut it out, fold it along the broken lines and stick it together, decorated with stripes and circular patterns. To finish it off, stick toothpicks firmly into the hole at the top to look like tent-poles. Transfer the diagram of the handcart onto thin cardboard, cut it out and stick it together. Stick the shaft on underneath the body, fix on the wheels, attach the seat, and the cart is finished.

For the cradle, transfer the two ends and the centre onto card. Fold the centre section along the broken lines, and stick the end pieces on. The quilt and pillow section merely lie loosely in the cradle.

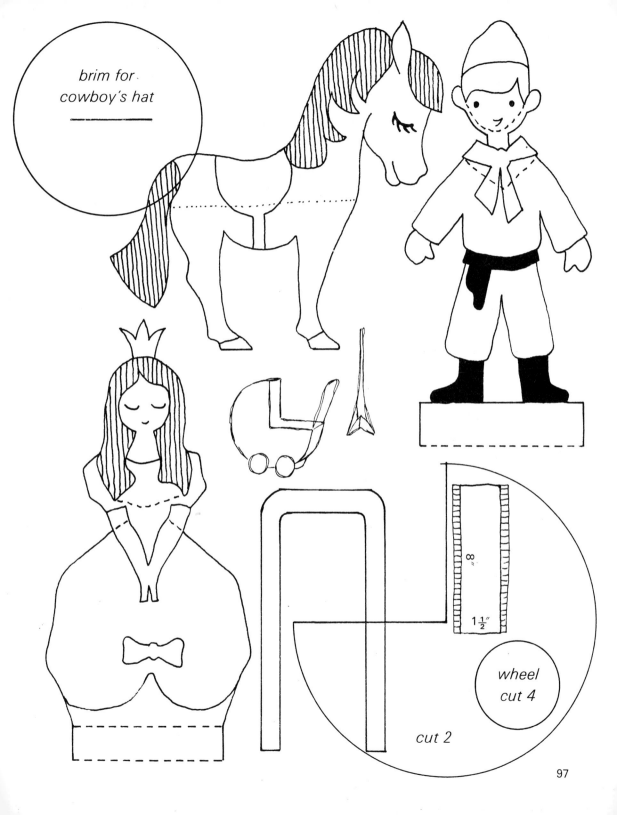

brim for
cowboy's hat

8"

1 1/2"

wheel
cut 4

cut 2

97

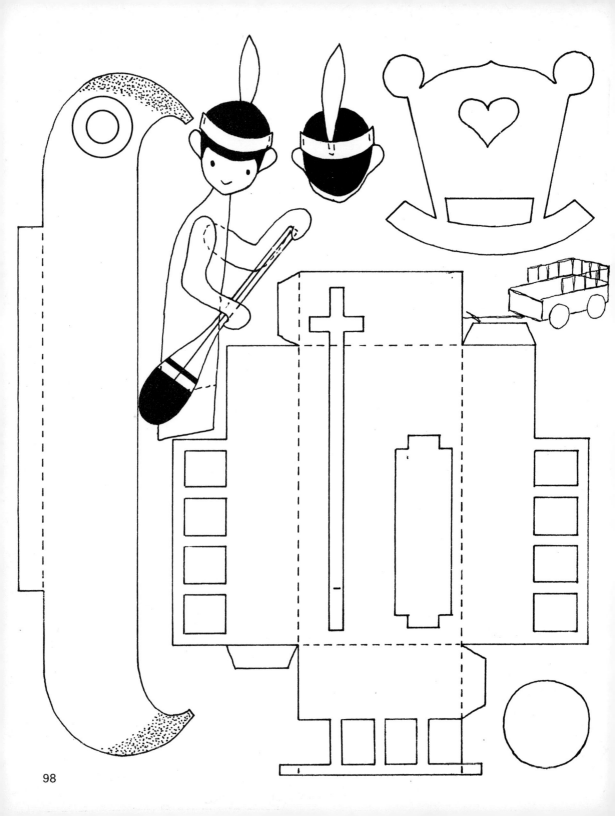

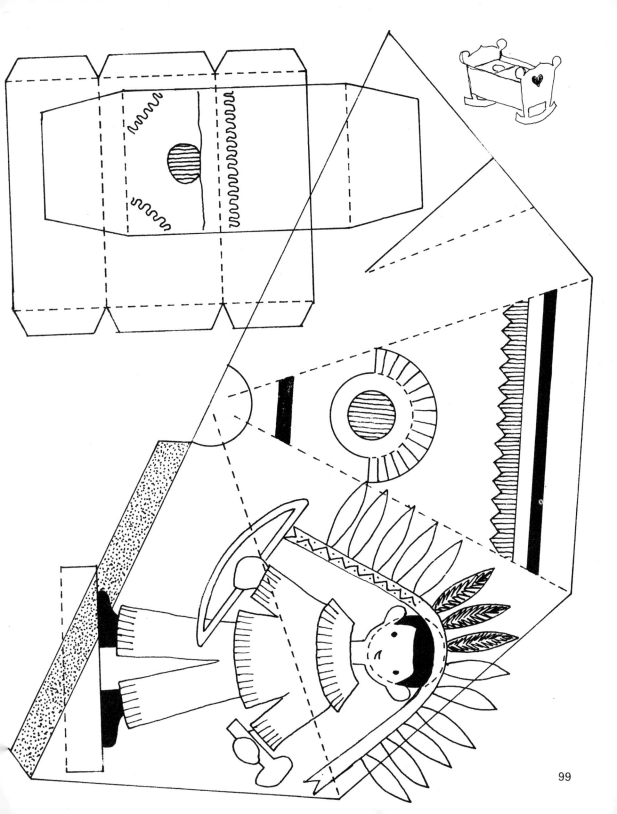

99

Giraffe and dromedary

Transfer the front and hind sections of the giraffe onto a piece of strong white cardboard. Paint on the brown patches and cut out both sections. The body is drawn and painted on a piece of thin white paper, which is cut out and stuck onto a cardboard tube from a roll of paper towels. The size of the tube must suit the body-size of the giraffe and the dromedary (the circumference being indicated by the dotted circle on the dromedary). If the roll is too big, then the body piece must be enlarged to correspond. Push a pipe-cleaner through the little hole in the front section, leaving only about $\frac{1}{8}$ inch for the knot. Brush paste round the edge of the front section, and apply it to the body section so that the pipe-cleaner sticks up through the centre of the tube. Now paste the hind end of the body section, and push the remainder of the pipe-cleaner through the little hole in the hind section. Hold the three sections still until the paste is dry and they are firmly fixed together. Bend the tail into shape, cut it to a suitable length and dip the tip into brown paint.

The dromedary is made of brown card, or brown paper pasted onto card, and is assembled in the same way as the giraffe. The centre body section is cut double and the upper part stuck together as far as the broken line. The top of the hump has a tuft of sewing-cotton stuck between the two layers of paper. Now the whole thing is ready to be stuck onto a piece of paper-towel roll.

100

101

Penguin

The penguin is made from double-sided black paper, or from two sheets stuck together, if only one side is black. Transfer the shape onto the paper and cut it out. The wings and breast are made of white paper and stuck to the body as shown on the diagram. Roll the body into shape: do not make any sharp folds. Fix the wings together with two staples at the back. Now bend the head and wings forward and stick them to the body as shown in the diagram. Cut the beak and the feet from orange paper, fold them and stick them on.

beak

paste

feet

103

Piggy bank

The big pigs in the picture are made from a cardboard tube $2\frac{1}{2}$ inches in diameter and a smaller one $1\frac{1}{2}$ inches in diameter. Cut a piece of the larger roll $3\frac{1}{2}$ inches long, and of the smaller roll, $\frac{1}{2}$ inch long. Cut a slot in the large tube, as shown in fig. 1. Cut the two end pieces from cardboard, following the heavy lines in fig. 2, making the round shape match the circumference of the cardboard tube. Stick the front and back sections to their own ends of the tube, so that the money slot is above the feet. Now cover the body and the two end sections in red paper, drawing along the dotted lines for the front end, to form the ears. The small tube (the snout) is closed at one end with a disc of cardboard (fig. 3) and the whole thing covered, to

match, with red paper: one circle for the cardboard disc, and a piece for the snout itself, made as in fig. 4. The flaps on the snout are bent outwards and pasted, to fix the snout to the centre of the head. Cut out two nostrils in white and two eyes in black and stick them on. Stick on a spiral of white paper for the tail; the dotted area shows where the paste should go.

The pig's back can be decorated in many different ways. The three little pigs in the picture are: **A.** red, with white spots of various sizes, **B.** orange with two red hearts, **C.** green, with a yellow lacy cut-out (see fig. 5). Fold a circle of paper 4 times and cut out the shaded areas.

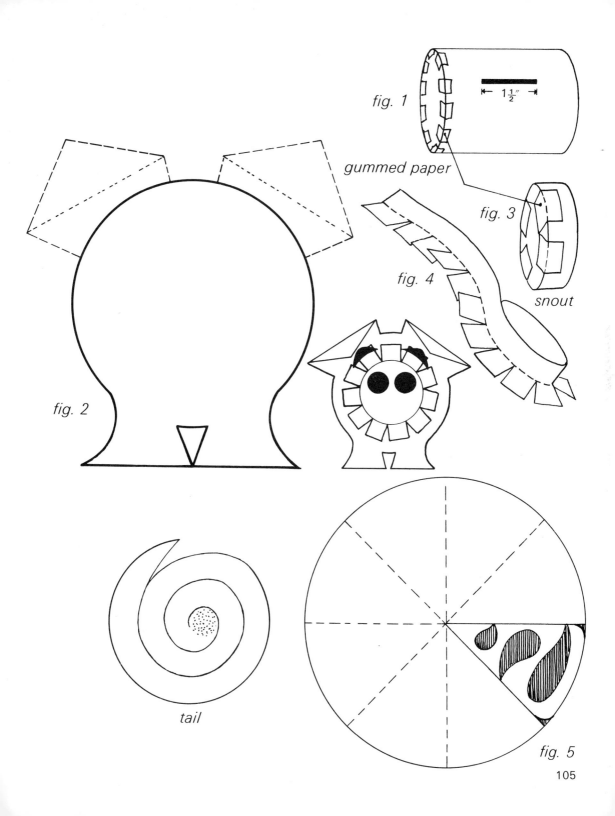

fig. 1

$1\frac{1}{2}''$

gummed paper

fig. 2

fig. 3

fig. 4

snout

tail

fig. 5

105

careful not to form a sharp fold (follow the diagram here). Fold one corner under and roll the paper strip up with little tucks, so that the rose looks full and beautiful. Turn the last corner down and fold it in. Twist about 6 inches of fine wire around the base, and the rose is ready. For larger roses, cut the tissue paper strips a little longer and wider.

The tree: mix the plaster and pour it into the plant-pot. Stand the stake upright in it and let it set. Cut the polystyrene to size and set it on the stake. Stick the roses into the polystyrene, beginning at the bottom, against the stake. When all the roses are fixed, cut some leaves from green tissue paper. Fold them, put a dab of paste on the outer side and tuck them between two roses, or wherever there may be a small gap.

For the garland, plait a braid of 3×10 strands of cotton, making the length suit the wearer. Twist the roses onto the braid, one at a time, from the outer side, making sure that they touch each other. Cut a ribbon of green tissue paper, doubled, the same length as the garland. Cut out the leaves, as shown in the diagram, and stick them to the inner side of the garland. Bend the leaves outwards, and stick them firmly to the roses.

Rose tree and rose garland

The materials for the roses are: coloured tissue paper, fine wire and paste; for the tree: a yoghurt carton or a small plastic flower-pot with a piece of silver foil at the bottom, a flower-stake about 12 inches long, a piece of expanded polystyrene and a little plaster.

The roses for both tree and garland are made as follows: cut the tissue paper into strips $10\frac{1}{2} \times \frac{3}{4}$ inches and stick the long edges together, being

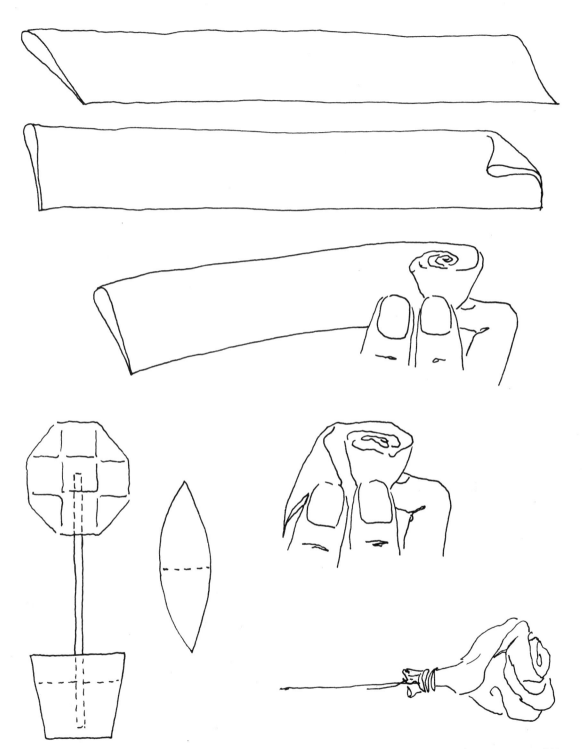

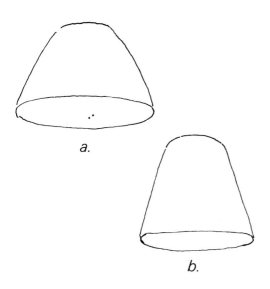

Things made from egg cartons

These two diagrams show one cup *a* from the base of the carton, and one *b* from the lid. These two letters are used throughout on the diagrams.

When the various objects are to be painted, this should be done before they are assembled. Put them into lukewarm water for a minute, take them out and lay them on a newspaper. They are easiest to paint while they are still a little moist. If several objects are to be made, the sections can be dipped into plastic paint, not too thick, and laid to dry on a newspaper.

a.

b.

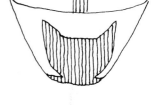

The cat

Transfer the shapes onto *a* cups, cut them out, paint them and stick them together.

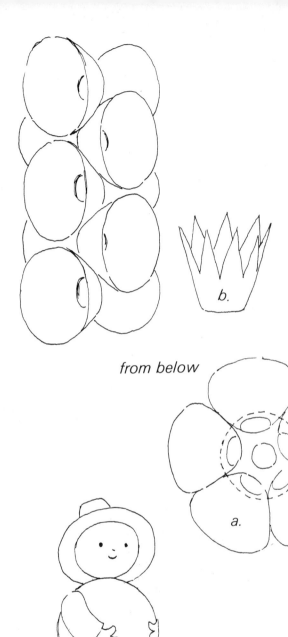

Long ornament

The length of the ornament can be varied to suit your needs. Stick *a* cups together in pairs, hour-glass fashion, remembering that they need to be painted on the inside. Stick the hour-glasses together, as in the diagram, using quick-drying glue. Cut some *b* cups into points along the edge, and stick one into each *a* cup. You can add a little Styrofoam ball (about an inch in diameter) inside that again. Instead of being painted, the cups can have kitchen foil folded over them, but this does make them rather more difficult to stick together.

b.

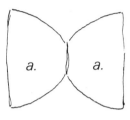

a. *a.*

from below

a.

from above

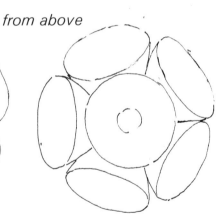

Table decoration

Stick six *a* cups together, as shown in the diagram, remembering to paint them inside. Decorate the side cups with tiny coloured Styrofoam balls, to look like Easter eggs, or stick a *b* cup, cut into points, into each *a* cup. A little man can be set on top; he is made of two Styrofoam balls, about 1 and 2 inches in diameter, fixed together with a tooth-pick. Give him arms, and a hat with a brim, cut from a *b* cup. Two of these bases can be stuck together to make a sphere (see the diagram on the next page).

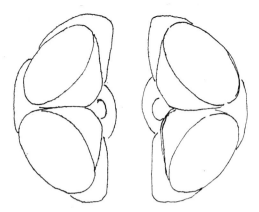

Stick a *b* cup, cut into points, into each *a* cup, and, if desired, a small Styrofoam ball. Attach the string before the two halves are stuck together. You could use elastic thread instead of string.

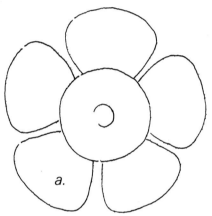

a.

from below

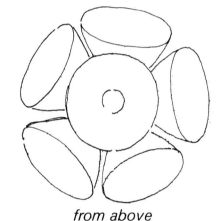

from above

This decoration is similar to the previous one, but it is rather easier to stick together. First stick two *a* cups, hour-glass fashion, then stick five *a* cups firmly onto the bottom half of the hour-glass (see diagram). Decorate it as described for the first one.

from the side

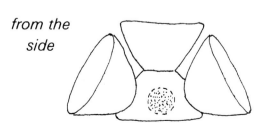

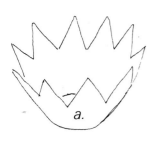

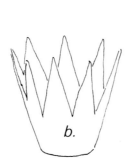

Candlesticks

Stick together five *a* cups and five *b* cups, all cut into points around the edge, as shown in the diagram. Insert a candle-holder and a candle. Flowers can be made in much the same way as the candlesticks (see diagram). Paint some cups and some Styrofoam balls, and assemble them into a flower with a tooth-pick. Set them in a piece of expanded polystyrene and the decoration is ready.

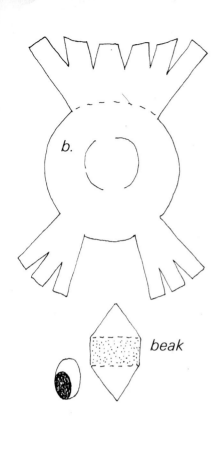

Birds

The birds are cut as shown in the diagram, painted and stuck together (see the diagram again). The eyes and beak for the perching birds are cut from paper and stuck on. Make five or six birds and set them on a piece of cardboard, to look like a flock of chattering sparrows.

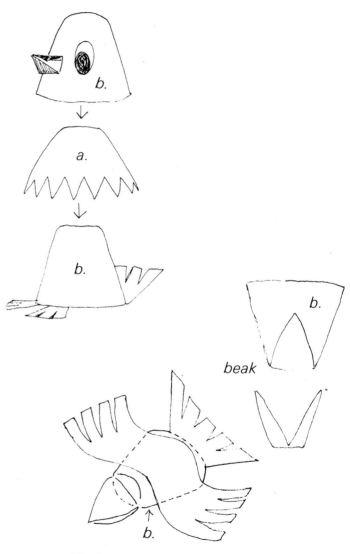

beak

The flying bird is hung by a thread from the spot on its back. The beak is the bottom of a *b* cup, folded together.

113

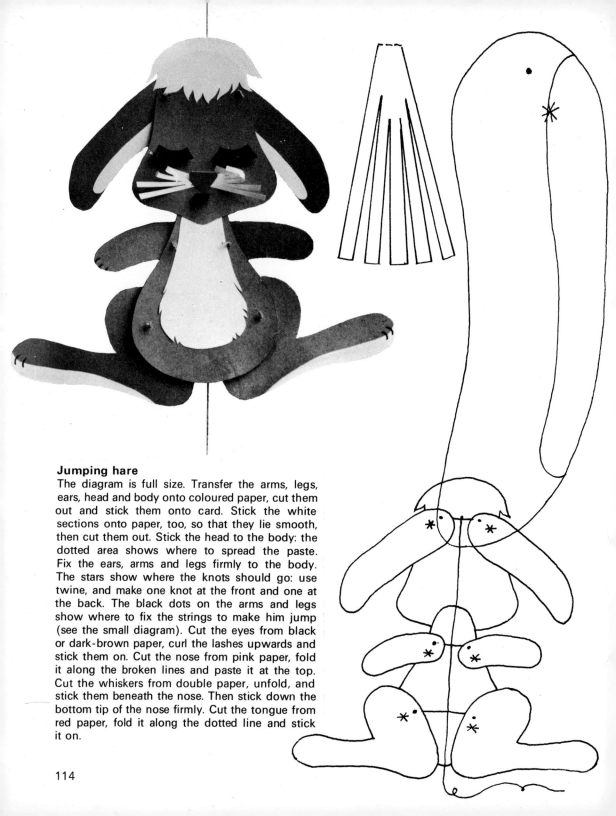

Jumping hare

The diagram is full size. Transfer the arms, legs, ears, head and body onto coloured paper, cut them out and stick them onto card. Stick the white sections onto paper, too, so that they lie smooth, then cut them out. Stick the head to the body: the dotted area shows where to spread the paste. Fix the ears, arms and legs firmly to the body. The stars show where the knots should go: use twine, and make one knot at the front and one at the back. The black dots on the arms and legs show where to fix the strings to make him jump (see the small diagram). Cut the eyes from black or dark-brown paper, curl the lashes upwards and stick them on. Cut the nose from pink paper, fold it along the broken lines and paste it at the top. Cut the whiskers from double paper, unfold, and stick them beneath the nose. Then stick down the bottom tip of the nose firmly. Cut the tongue from red paper, fold it along the dotted line and stick it on.

114

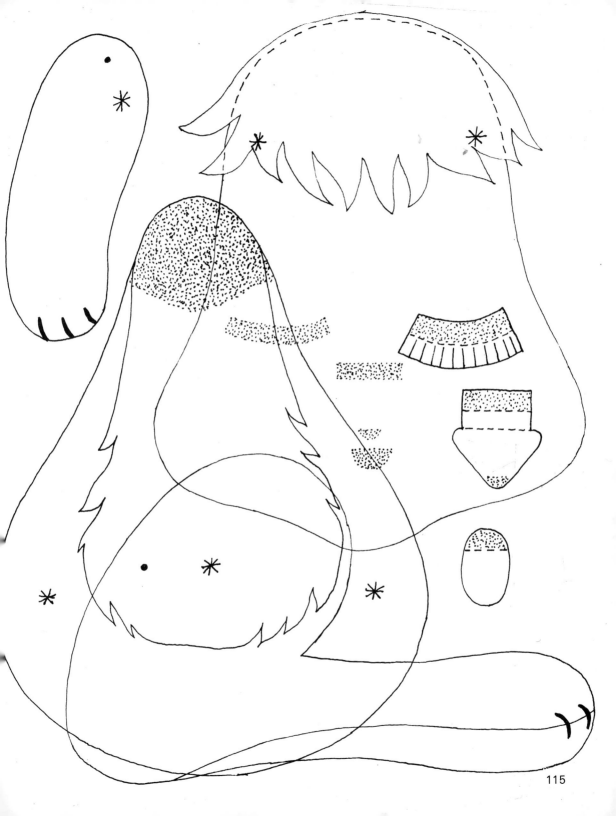

Cut-out paper pictures

Trace the whole picture onto a piece of grease-proof paper. Transfer the individual parts: dress, trousers, hat, cauldron, etc., onto coloured paper and cut them out. It gives a very gay effect if you cut some sections from a dress- or carpet-catalogue.

Now transfer the outline onto a piece of thin white paper, and stick on all the parts firmly. Cut out the completed picture, leaving a thin white edging all round. Stick the picture onto a sheet of stiff, tinted cardboard, about 8 × 9 inches.

A light to relax by

Use a sheet of strong cardboard, 30 × 8 inches, in white or a pale colour. Make a plan with the given dimensions, following fig. *a*. Cut along the unbroken lines, score along the broken lines and fold. Stick the two short edges together. Fold the two curved flaps from each side inwards towards the middle, and stick them together where they overlap. Trace the top and bottom sections to the given dimensions, cut them out and stick them on (fig. *b*). This lamp-shade is held by the electric socket itself, so that the bulb hangs where the flaps are stuck together. The little flaps in the top are bent upwards, to allow the heat from the bulb to escape.

Dotted areas show where to put the paste.

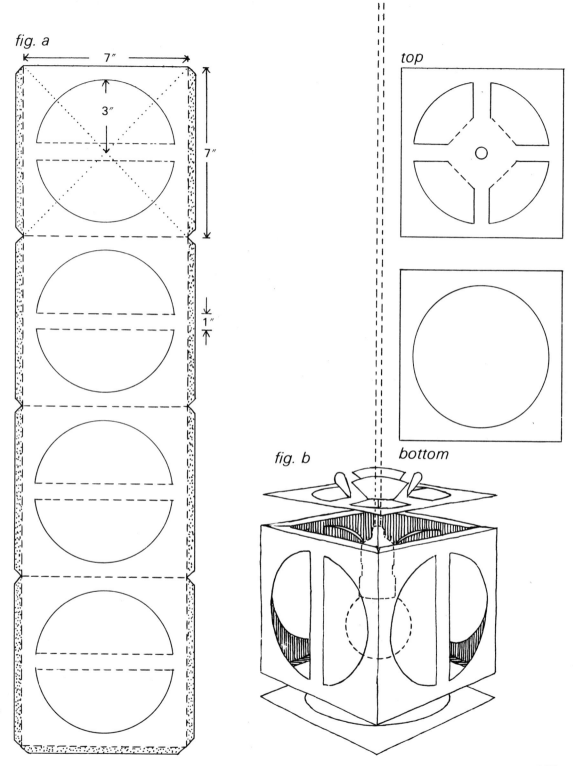

fig. a

7″

3″

7″

1″

top

bottom

fig. b

E

C

B

A

D

Lacy cut-outs

All the cut-outs are made from coloured tissue paper, two or three layers stuck together. They are intended to be hung at the window on a thread, so that the light can really play on the colours. Done in gold or silver paper, the cut-outs can also be used as doilies.

All the diagrams are full size, and planned for transferring onto folded paper.

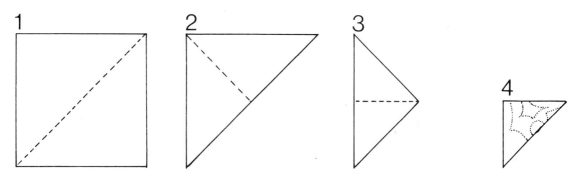

A. Fold a piece of pale-lilac tissue paper, 7 inches square, as shown in figs 1, 2, 3, 4. Transfer the pattern onto the one-eighth section, and cut away the shaded portions. Fold and cut out a sheet of deep lilac in the same way. Unfold the cut-outs and stick them together, rotating one pattern through 45°.

B. Fold two pieces of light-green tissue paper, $3\frac{1}{2}$ inches square, across the middle. Transfer the pattern onto both pieces, so that the broken line lies along the fold. Cut away the shaded sections, unfold the paper and stick the two pieces together, with the axes at right-angles to each other.

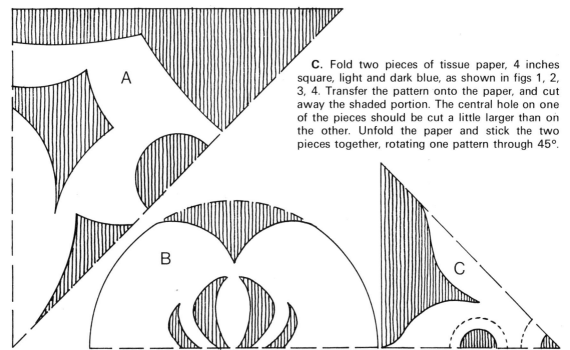

C. Fold two pieces of tissue paper, 4 inches square, light and dark blue, as shown in figs 1, 2, 3, 4. Transfer the pattern onto the paper, and cut away the shaded portion. The central hole on one of the pieces should be cut a little larger than on the other. Unfold the paper and stick the two pieces together, rotating one pattern through 45°.

D. Fold two pieces of pink tissue paper, 7 inches square, as shown in figs 1, 2, 3, 4. Transfer one of the two patterns, D1 or D2, onto each piece of tissue paper. Cut away the shaded portions and stick the two sheets together, so that the circular hole lies directly over the star.

E. This consists of three different cut-outs in red, blue and mauve tissue paper, 7 inches square. Fold each of the three sheets of paper as in figs 1, 2, 3, 4, and transfer the separate patterns onto the sheets. Cut away the shaded portions and unfold the paper. Stick the three cut-outs together, so that the holes form a line towards the centre.

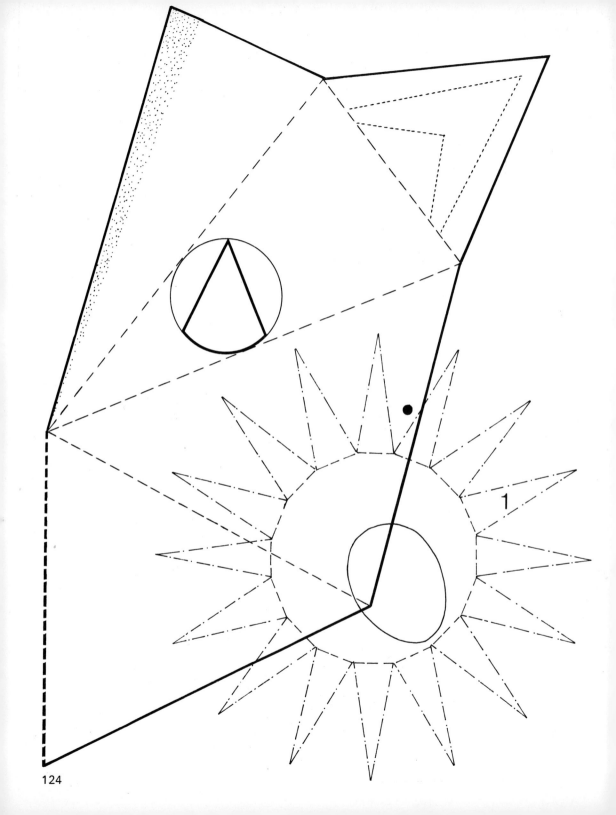

Cat mask

The mask is made from a sheet of thin, black cardboard. It is cut out double, since the card is folded along the dotted line, downwards from the muzzle. The easiest way of transferring the diagram onto black cardboard is, first, to trace the diagram off onto grease-proof paper, then to scribble a layer of chalk on the back, and draw off the diagram onto the card. Cut out the shape, score along the dotted lines, and fold, so that the muzzle sticks out when the mask is pasted together upwards from the muzzle. Cut out the eye triangles, and stick two small, green half-moons on each eye. The dotted shape in the ears is cut from either gold or white paper and stuck on; the ears themselves are bent forwards a little. Bend four pipe-cleaners and stitch them to the centre of the muzzle. Fix elastic between the two holes in the sides.

Owl mask

Transfer the thick, unbroken lines onto a piece of strong brown paper. Cut out the pattern double, folding the paper and laying the dotted line to the fold. For the eye-stars, cut two each of 1, 2 and 3, in brown, orange and black paper, respectively. Bend the points forward along the dotted lines. Now stick the stars to the mask, aligning the eye-holes in each of the four sections. Cut the large triangle for the beak from gold paper and stick it on. The eye-circles of the mask itself are inclined towards the beak. Fix an elastic between the holes in each side.

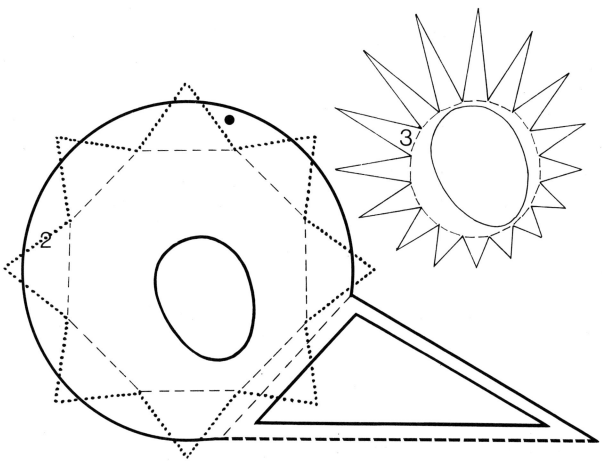